THE ROMFORD
OUTRAGE

THE ROMFORD OUTRAGE

OUTRAGE

The Murder of
Inspector Thomas Simmons, 1885

Linda Rhodes
and Kathryn Abnett

First published in Great Britain in 2009 by
Wharncliffe Local History
an imprint of
Pen & Sword Books Ltd
47 Church Street
Barnsley
South Yorkshire
S70 2AS

ISBN 978 1 84563 076 8

A CIP catalogue record for this book is available
from the British Library

Printed by the MPG Books Group
in the UK

Pen & Sword Books Ltd incorporates the Imprints of
Pen & Sword Aviation, Pen & Sword Family History,
Pen & Sword Maritime, Pen & Sword Military, Wharncliffe Local History,
Pen & Sword Select, Pen & Sword Military Classics, Leo Cooper,
Remember When, Seaforth Publishing and Frontline Publishing

For a complete list of Pen & Sword titles please contact
PEN & SWORD BOOKS LIMITED
47 Church Street, Barnsley, South Yorkshire, S70 2AS, England
E-mail: enquiries@pen-and-sword.co.uk
Website: www.pen-and-sword.co.uk

Contents

List of Illustrations

Acknowledgements

Our particular thanks are due to: Simon Donoghue (Havering Local Studies Library); Becky Latchford, Bryan Turner, Janet Lee & Fred Feather (all current or former staff and volunteers at the Essex Police Museum); Maggie Bird (Metropolitan Police Historical Collection); Roger Logan (Foresters Heritage Trust); Brian Norman; Lee Shelden; Bill George; Joan Burgoyne; Nancy Crisp; the late Sir Charles Graham, Bart, of Netherby Hall; Nigel Rixson, Kevin Trott.

We would also like to acknowledge the assistance given by the staff of the following:
Essex Record Office; National Archives; British Library Newspaper Library; Cumbria Record Office; Library of the Middle Temple.

Introduction:
'Courage and Coolness'

It was approaching five o'clock on the morning of Friday, 2 January 1874 as the figure of a top-hatted policeman trudged slowly along South Street, in the town of Romford in Essex. The 29-year-old Constable Thomas Simmons had already been on duty for about seven hours. He had patrolled alone, occasionally meeting fellow officers at prearranged times to exchange information. He must have been looking forward to reporting back to the police station in the Market Place in a couple of hours' time, before enjoying some well-earned sleep at his home in Victoria Road.

Simmons raised his lantern and moved it from side to side so that its rays illuminated the door and windows of the Post Office. All was well, so Simmons turned away, ready to move on. His eye suddenly caught movement at the crossroads about fifty yards ahead, where South Street met the High Street. Two figures were striding across the junction, in the direction of London, with large bundles slung across their shoulders. Simmons was immediately suspicious and set off in pursuit. He caught up with them on the outskirts of town, where the High Street became London Road.

'Where are you going?' he asked.

The pair, both young men, ignored him and walked on. Simmons ran past and turned round to face them.

'What are you carrying?' he demanded, looking at the bundles wrapped in rugs and curtains.

Still no answer. Suddenly one of the men threw his bundle at Simmons's head, while the other tripped him up. The officer was left flat on his face in the mud while the pair sprinted away with the second bundle.

Undaunted, Simmons hauled himself back to his feet and resumed the chase. He caught up once again and seized their collars, but they fought back fiercely. One punched Simmons several times in the face, forcing him to let go in order to defend himself. The second scooped up handfuls of mud from the road and pushed it into Simmons's face, forcing it into his eyes and mouth. Despite this, Simmons managed to handcuff one of the men to himself. He also snatched the remaining bundle, which the second man tried without success to wrench away before giving up and disappearing into the darkness. Simmons then began to drag his captive towards the police station, stopping to pick up the second bundle on the way. The man did not go willingly, but repeatedly threw himself down on the ground and tried to trip Simmons up. Eventually, however, the mud-splattered officer forced the young man through the doors of the police station.

The culprit was locked in a cell and the bundles unwrapped. Simmons and his colleagues gazed in wonder as objects came tumbling out: silver-plated cutlery, candlesticks, a glass vase, an ivory box, embroidered tablecloths, muslin curtains, items of clothing, a coffee-pot. Where had the objects come from, they wondered? The puzzle was solved at about a quarter to seven that morning, when a milkman on his round noticed signs of a break-in at the house of Captain William Jesse Coope at Brook Street Hill, near Brentwood, about five miles from Romford.

The burglars, the second of whom was captured a few weeks later, were brothers named Golborne from Blackwall in London's Docklands. The exploits of Simmons in outfighting two criminals and recapturing their haul were widely

High Street, Romford, sketched by Alfred Bennett Bamford in 1884. *London Borough of Havering Local Studies*

publicized, and he became the hero of the hour. A testimonial fund was set up for him, one contributor being the judge at the trial of one of the burglars, who put in £5 from court funds. The Chief Constable of the Essex Constabulary presented Simmons with the Merit Star, given only to a select band of officers who had displayed 'highly distinguished and discreet conduct in the discharge of duty particularly when accompanied with risk of life, personal courage and coolness aided by marked intelligence'.

Eleven years later Thomas Simmons, now promoted to the rank of inspector and in charge not only of Romford but the entire Liberty of Havering-atte-Bower, was to tackle suspected burglars once more. This time, however, the outcome would not be a successful capture, but his murder in cold blood. This is the story of the crime and the manhunt which followed, culminating in another police killing, this time in the far north of England.

I
'In Romford to Dwell'

Thomas Simmons was born on Sunday, 22 December 1844 at Weeley Heath in north-east Essex. His father, also Thomas, was an agricultural labourer from the neighbouring parish of Little Clacton, and his mother Sarah, formerly Moor, hailed from Boxted.[1] Thomas was the couple's first child, and was eventually joined by brothers Harry, Charles, Ralph (or Aracher) and Frederick, and sisters Sarah and Mary.

Weeley, ten miles from Colchester, was described in White's 1848 *Directory of Essex* as 'a pleasant village, chiefly in one street'. Weeley Heath, on the eastern fringes of the village, was by a quirk of boundaries actually situated on a finger of land belonging to the parish of St Osyth. Extensive military barracks had once stood on the heath, only to be demolished after the end of the Napoleonic Wars in 1815. By the time of the 1861 census Thomas, at 16 years of age, was

Thomas Simmons's appointment to the Essex Constabulary, 1865. *Essex Police Museum*

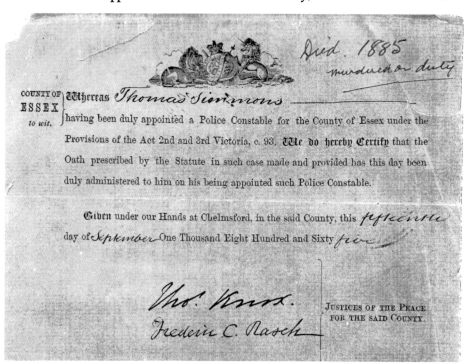

employed at a local flour mill. He later worked for his father, now a small farmer and basket-maker. By the summer of 1865 Simmons, in common with many rural labourers, had grown tired of enduring long hours of strenuous work for pitifully low wages, and applied to join the police force. He travelled to the Essex Constabulary headquarters at Springfield Court, north of Chelmsford, for an interview with the Chief Constable, John Bunch Bonnemaison McHardy. Born at Nassau in the Bahamas, and formerly a captain in the Royal Navy, McHardy had been appointed as the county's first Chief Constable back in 1840, after Essex had adopted the County Police Act of 1839 and set up a professional force along the lines of London's Metropolitan Police.

McHardy decided that Simmons was a suitable candidate, and handed him a form on which three referees had to certify that 'he is sober, honest, and of good temper, and that his connexions and associates are respectable'. Simmons first approached the Reverend William Yorick Smythies, of Hillside House in Weeley Heath. Smythies proclaimed that he had 'Never signed a recommendation with greater satisfaction'. The second referee was William Edward Thorpe, of Pond Farm, and the third was Thomas Grimwood, of Weeley Flour Mill, who had probably employed Simmons back in 1861. On 11 September 1865 police surgeon Daniel Manthorp examined Simmons and certified that he was 'fit for the Police Duty'. He was recorded as 21 years of age (in fact he was still only 20 at the time), 5 feet 9 inches tall, with dark brown hair, brown eyes, fair complexion, and could read and write well.

Four days later Simmons was once more in Chelmsford, this time to be sworn in before the magistrates at the Shire Hall. His warrant number was 1445. Another man taking the oath that day was 19-year-old George Samuel Chase, a native of Springfield, whose future career would intertwine with that of Simmons. The two new recruits had to supply themselves with 'a knapsack, agreeably to pattern, two pairs of white trowsers, two pairs of white gloves, and a decent suit of plain clothes'. The uniform consisted of a navy blue single-breasted frock-coat, its eight buttons marked 'Essex Constabulary'. On the collar was a silver embroidered crown alongside the officer's number. On top he would wear either a cape or waterproof greatcoat. The training, at the force headquarters, was rudimentary by today's standards, much time being spent on military-style foot drill. Simmons and Chase would have carefully studied *Orders and Instructions for the Government of the Essex Constabulary*, written by John McHardy himself. It was based on Metropolitan Police guidelines, and the first, rather startling, command was that 'Each man shall devote his whole time to the service of the Essex County Constabulary'. The trainees may also have been disquieted to read that 'A constable guilty of any neglect or violation of duty is liable to a penalty of ten pounds, or imprisonment with hard labour for a month'.

By mid-November 1865 the pair had satisfactorily completed the two-month probationary period. Simmons was given collar number 85. Its previous holder, ex-soldier Edward Ahern, had been forced to resign on account of 'want of sobriety'. He was one of countless officers disciplined or dismissed for drunkenness in the early years of the Essex force. In July 1840 a furious Chief Constable McHardy had noted in the Force Orders that three constables 'returning to Dunmow from a fair at Thaxted, entered a public house in direct violation of the 21st section of the 2nd Article of the Instructions, and actually danced in the said public house'.

For their first postings as constables 3rd class, both Simmons and Chase were sent to Romford. Pronounced 'Rumford', it was a market town of just under 5,000 inhabitants lying some twelve miles east of London on the great road built by the Romans to carry their armies into East Anglia. It grouped with the parishes of Havering-atte-Bower to the north and Hornchurch to the south to form the ancient Royal Liberty of Havering-atte-Bower, from which the present-day London Borough of Havering derives its identity.[2]

The south side of Romford Market Place in 1874, looking east. On the right is Denny Stone's draper's shop, founded in 1864. *London Borough of Havering Local Studies*

Stepping off the steam train from Chelmsford, the two may well have been assailed by the distinctive smell of malt, barley and hops emanating from the premises of the town's chief employer, the Ind Coope brewery. An officer meeting them on the platform then led them the quarter of a mile along South Street to the police station. At journey's end, there was no purpose-built facility as might now be expected in a busy town. Instead, Simmons and Chase were shown into the Court House, located at the western end of the Market Place, close to the crossroads of South Street and High Street. The police station occupied rooms on the ground floor of this building. Census returns show that, unusually for the times, no officers lived there. It did, however, have cells for the short-term housing of prisoners before they were brought before the magistrates. The Court House's upper floor was the venue for the weekly Petty Sessions, where magistrates dealt 'summary justice' for relatively minor offences, and until 1870 the three-monthly Quarter Sessions were also held there. It was also at that time the meeting place of Romford's Local Board, an early form of town council.

Simmons and Chase would soon have got to know their new colleagues. Inspector William Gilpin, born in County Armagh, Ireland, was in his late fifties and had served with the Essex Constabulary since 1842. Romford was part of the Brentwood Division, along with Billericay and Orsett. Inspector Gilpin's immediate superior was Superintendent William Bridges, another Irishman, who was based at Brentwood Police Station. Gilpin's right-hand man at Romford was Sergeant George Shead, aged 40 and from Cliffe in Kent, who had formerly served at Billericay.

Just before Christmas 1865, a month after arriving at Romford, Simmons celebrated his 21st birthday. In April 1866, after a general pay rise, his income rose from 17 shillings per week to 19 shillings. This was probably twice as much as he would have earned as an agricultural labourer, assuming that his father had paid him at all! In January 1866 a railway station had opened at Weeley, making it easier for Simmons to visit his parents on his rare days off.

His new environment at Romford would have been a vivid contrast to his quiet home village. Stepping out of the Court House when the main cattle and corn market was in full swing on Wednesdays, Simmons would have been surrounded by vibrancy, noise and colour; not for nothing, as local historian Brian Evans notes in his book *Bygone Romford*, had the town earned the nickname 'Blareum'. In 1247 Henry III had sealed a charter granting Romford a livestock market every Wednesday, and it had become one of the largest in the region. Writing in the early twentieth century, Charles Hussey noted that it offered 'dealers in every conceivable commodity, in old iron, in sponges, in harness, the

Another 1874 view of the south side of the Market Place, this time looking west. The Swan is in the centre of the picture. *London Borough of Havering Local Studies*

sweetstuff stall, the ropemaker and basket weaver, the purveyor of medicines both for man and beast, the agricultural implement maker, and the numerous buyers and sellers of poultry, horses, cattle, pigs, goats, sheep, and every domestic animal one could mention'.[3] Naturally this could mean rich pickings for many kinds of criminals, from pickpockets to cattle rustlers. Thomas Simmons was to become an acknowledged expert in horse-stealing cases, and would have gained this expertise during those early days at Romford.

The road passing through the centre of the Market Place was then the major highway from London to Colchester and the East Coast ports. It had witnessed many royal travellers. Elizabeth I passed through several times, for example on her way to spend the night at nearby Gidea Hall in 1568. In 1821 a royal funeral procession passed through, that of Queen Caroline, the estranged wife of George IV, heading for the port of Harwich en route to her native Brunswick. The coffin was stationary for some time in the Market Place, and there were moving scenes as people clustered round to touch it, and later to walk alongside carrying flaming torches. From the time of Edward the Confessor (to whom Romford's parish church was dedicated) until the sixteenth century, kings and queens of England and their entourages had often stayed at their palace, or hunting lodge, at Havering-atte-Bower. The people of Romford must have watched in awe as the royal carriages and mounted escorts moved slowly along the High Street and turned left into North Street for the final leg of their journey from the capital.

A less exalted resident was the notorious Captain Thomas Blood, said to have lodged over an apothecary's shop in the Market Place, who stole the Crown Jewels from the Tower of London in 1671. He was captured soon afterwards, but was controversially pardoned by King Charles II and even given a pension of £500 per year. Blood did not survive long to enjoy his new-found riches, and was buried at St Margaret's Church, Westminster, under an epitaph ending with 'Let's rejoice his time was come to die'.

Before the coming of the railway in 1839, forty stage coaches went through Romford every day, many making scheduled stops to change horses. On being introduced to the landlords of the numerous Market Place inns, Simmons might have noticed that some of the older buildings still retained the ambience of those glory days. The Dolphin, for example, dating from the early 1600s, is described as having a galleried courtyard as well as extensive stables.

The town could boast a plethora of watering holes to service the needs of the thirsty traveller. Among the numerous pubs on the south side of the Market Place was the ancient Windmill and Bells, behind which lay a horse-slaughtering yard. Also on the south side was the Swan (sometimes called the White Swan), partly dating from 1594. A giant plaster swan dangled from its roof. Two doors down from the Swan was the Blücher's Head, commemorating that Prussian Field Marshal's aid to Wellington in the defeat of Napoleon at Waterloo (during the First World War its name would be changed to the Duke of Wellington to appease anti-German sentiment). The nearby King's Arms dated from Elizabethan times.

Two pubs on the north side of the Market Place that Simmons would have known are, happily, still in existence. One is the Lamb, which stood immediately opposite the Court House. It had been rebuilt after a fire of 1852. In 1871 the Lamb was in the hands of 62-year-old widow Mary Wendon and her son Charles. The second survivor, the Cock and Bell, dating from the fifteenth century, stands adjacent to St Edward's churchyard and is now known as the Church House.

Simmons may have been surprised to discover that St Edward's Church itself was one of the newest buildings in the Market Place. Opened in 1850, it had replaced the original church of 1410. It did not please everyone. In 1880 George Terry, in his *Memories of Old Romford*, wrote that 'some persons were aggrieved at the fantastic gargoyles which are here and there to be seen projecting from the building'. A local wit had even written a satire which included the lines:

One would think the projector had been into hell,
Seen devils and fiends in despair;

St Andrew's Church, Romford, where Thomas Simmons married in 1868. *London Borough of Havering Local Studies*

And again was permitted in Romford to dwell,
And cut their likenesses there.

Do they think that these figures so hideous and strange,
Will attract poor people to prayer,
Or will they not rather with terror derange,
And frighten them into despair?

When Simmons walked beyond the eastern end of the Market Place he found himself amidst buildings that were less than twenty years old. This was Laurie Town, described in *Francis Frith's Romford* as 'the country's first garden city' and a 'revolutionary town planning project'. It had been the brainchild of Scotsman John Laurie, former high steward of the Liberty of Havering-atte-Bower. Laurie Square, also called St Edward's Square, contained four semi-detached villas, providing eight large town houses which in 1871 were home to a little colony of members of the clerical and medical professions. Alfred Wright, a 31-year-old GP, lived close to Philip Lugar, a retired surgeon. Their neighbours included William Skilton, rector of St Andrew's Church; Alfred Roberts, curate of Romford; and Joseph William Wright Drew, priest of St Edward's Catholic Church. The development also included some smaller houses and two public halls, St Edward's Hall and Laurie Hall. The latter, built around 1852, was originally intended to replace the Court House but was used instead as an entertainment venue (according to local tradition, Charles Dickens once gave a public reading there) and home of the Literary & Mechanics' Institute. John Laurie himself left Romford in the late 1850s, having been elected MP for Barnstaple in Devon in 1854. The Laurie Town development never reached the scale he had originally intended, and after his death in 1864 it was put up for sale.

Towards the end of 1866 a shocking discovery was made at the bridge where the Battis footpath, which ran alongside the railway, crossed the River Rom at Waterloo Road, about a quarter of a mile from the railway station. A hat and umbrella lay on the bloodstained ground, and when a passer-by picked up the hat and turned it over, fresh blood ran out over his hand. The police had begun dragging the river when news came through that the body of a middle-aged man with terrible throat wounds had been found further downstream. He was identified as Simon Godfrey, brother of the high bailiff of Romford County Court. Murder was naturally suspected, but the case turned out to be, in the words of the *Essex Times*, one of 'shocking and determined suicide'. Mr Godfrey, depressed due to financial problems, had slashed his throat eleven times with a razor and then plunged into the water to drown.

Thomas Simmons was promoted to constable 2nd class on 1 April 1867. With a secure, respected job and the reasonable income of 21 shillings per week, he was now in a position to consider marriage. His chosen bride, Mary Ann Jennings, had been born in February 1844 at Downham, near Billericay in Essex, making her a few months older than Thomas. They were both the eldest of large families, and came from similar backgrounds. Mary Ann's father William Jennings, originally from East Hanningfield, was an agricultural labourer who rose to become a farm bailiff.

Simmons and Mary Ann were married on Tuesday, 1 September 1868. The ceremony took place at St Andrew's Church, built only five years previously to the west of the town centre. Patricia Pound notes in her book *Romford Pubs* that St Andrew's was 'often called the Brewery Church because of strong brewery connections. The Coope family, the Inds, and other eminent brewery families worshipped there alongside their employees.' One of the witnesses to the wedding was William Elms, 42, a colleague of Simmons. PC Elms, born in Suffolk, had been a valet in a country house before joining the police in 1854. The other witness was 22-year-old Emily Jennings, a sister of the bride. When Thomas and Mary Ann returned to St Andrew's Church in June the following year for the baptism of their first child, the baby was given the names Emily Edith, no doubt in honour of her aunt.

2

'Gained the Good Will of All'

Before he married, Simmons would have rented a room in a private house or above a shop. He and his bride were no doubt delighted to take possession of a modern home, I Alma Cottages, in Victoria Road, next to a grocer's shop run by Amos Dodwell and not far from the Victoria pub. Together with Western and Eastern Roads, Victoria Road had been laid out in the 1850s. The area was summed up as follows in 1867 in this extract from an entertaining verse by M Q Donagan entitled 'Our Town: by a Townsman of Romford':

> We have a pleasant suburb on freehold land near to the Railway Station,
> It is quite a rising place, forming a most desirable and healthy habitation.[4]

Simmons would have worked a nine-hour shift at night, the starting and finishing times staggered according to the season, plus a further three hours during the day at the police station or patrolling the busy streets. On a typical spring evening he would have pulled on his top hat and bade goodbye to Mary Ann

Victoria Road, Romford. Thomas and Mary Ann Simmons lived in one of the houses on the extreme right of the picture. *London Borough of Havering Local Studies*

and baby Emily at about 8.40 pm. Using the 1871 census and contemporary trade directories, we can obtain a picture of people and places he may have encountered while walking to the police station to report for duty.

Almost immediately opposite the Simmons house stood the Victoria Steam Flour Mill, close to the junction of Victoria Road and South Street. A nearby windmill had, sadly, fallen into disuse when the high railway embankment cut off the wind supply to its sails. Simmons, as we know, had worked in a mill as a youth in Weeley, so he may have paused for a brief chat with the proprietor Henry Whitmore or his foreman miller John Gunn. Simmons then took a footpath around the mill, which cut off the corner and emerged by the Rising Sun in South Street. He was now at the railway station – a place he would have known well, as the Chief Constable ordered that officers should observe passengers getting on and off trains. This was a sensible practice in Romford, for whilst the opening of the railway in 1839 had ensured the area's expansion and future prosperity, it also meant that a relatively short and inexpensive journey now linked the town with London's impoverished and crime-ridden East End.

This particular evening Simmons strode under the brick railway arch, ignoring the slope on his left leading up to the ticket office and platforms. He then passed the line of horse-drawn cabs awaiting fares outside the Star, named after the earlier Star in the High Street, where Edward Ind had founded his brewery back in 1799. As Simmons hurried on past the gas works on his left, the county court building would have come into view on the other side of the road. It had opened in 1858 to deal with matters of civil law such as debts or boundary disputes, and was described in a contemporary newspaper as being in 'the surburban villa style . . . built with white brick facings, rustic quoins, and handsome brick mould cornices'. As we have seen, the Liberty of Havering Quarter Sessions had been transferred here in 1870, so Simmons would occasionally have been called upon to give evidence at the trials.

South Street was at this point tree-lined and largely residential. Simmons passed on his left six spacious semi-detached houses, one of which was the home of Charles Godfrey, high bailiff of the County Court. Western Road now branched off to the right. At its corner lay Stewards farmhouse, a whitewashed building in spacious grounds. Its name derived from the manor of Stewards, which had once extended across to Squirrels Heath, almost a mile to the east. Most of its land was now being built upon. Victoria Road, where Simmons lived, was one of many roads carved out of the Stewards estate. Stewards Manor House, as distinct from the farmhouse, had been demolished long before. Its most famous resident had been the metaphysical poet Francis Quarles, born there in 1592. On the site of the old

The Golden Lion, drawn by A B Bamford in 1889. *London Borough of Havering Local Studies*

mansion there now stood the red-brick Romford Hall, described in the Cornell Manuscript of 1908 as 'the most conspicuous and important building in South Street'. In 1871 it was the residence of North Surridge, 64, a solicitor and insurance agent. Adjacent to Romford Hall were Bosworth's Cottages, so-called because they were owned by a charity founded by Joseph Bosworth in his will of 1730. On the opposite side of the road, set back beyond its own drive, was The Lodge, a large modern house inhabited by Edmund Vipan Ind, a son of the founder of Ind Coope.

The character of South Street now changed once more, shops appearing on either side as the town centre grew closer. Simmons was now approaching the crossroads where South Street met the High Street and Market Place. At its north-western side stood the Golden Lion, dating from about 1450 and still surviving today. Turning right into the Market Place, Simmons would have entered the Court House and lined up on parade alongside his fellow constables. Inspector Gilpin checked that their uniforms were tidy and boots clean of mud, and read out any Force Orders received that day. The inspection over, the constables filed out and made their way to their respective beats. Some who worked in outlying districts

Inspector Gilpin (centre, with the double row of buttons), Sergeant Dennis and the Romford constables outside the Court House in the early 1870s. It is highly likely that Thomas Simmons is one of the group. *Ian Wilkes*

were taken there in a horse and trap. As we have seen, the men patrolled alone and on foot. Unlike some of their Metropolitan Police counterparts, Essex constables were not armed with cutlasses or firearms. Their only means of protection were a truncheon (painted with the county arms) and a rattle with which to raise the alarm if need be. A modicum of back-up was afforded by the sergeant who would tour the beats from time to time during the night in the horse and trap.

As time passed, Simmons gained a thorough knowledge of Romford's streets, side-alleys and courtyards, shops and pubs, and became a familiar figure to all its inhabitants. Sometimes he would patrol the High Street, leading west from the police station. An early stop might be the White Hart on the left, at least two centuries old by that time and Romford's busiest coaching inn. A few paces further on was the entrance to the brewery, described by M Q Donagan in 1867:

> The extensive brewery of Messrs Ind and Coope, is the principal feature of our town,
> And the excellence of their ales and stout, has obtained a far-famed renown.
> They have a rifle corps, two excellent bands, and annually the employees have a treat . . .

Occasionally the police would be called to cases of alleged pilfering by brewery employees. In May 1874 Simmons and Sergeant Dennis found some men in possession of hop pockets (large hessian sacks) clearly marked 'I.C. & Co'. The brewery manager lived close by in a large double-fronted building named Queen's House, so-called because Princess Charlotte of Mecklenberg-Strelitz had stopped there for coffee in 1761 on her journey to London to marry George III. The High Street passed across the River Rom by the brewery. After heavy rains the water level sometimes caused anxiety, and with good reason. M Q Donagan wittily sums up the river as follows:

> There's the River Rom, flows sometimes through our town – a lazy fellow who seldom labours,
> He's mostly confined to his bed, replete with filth, and a nuisance to all his neighbours.
> 'Tis not 'Flow on thou shining river', with him he's in odour most unpleasant,
> And offensive alike to the olfactory nerve of either prince or peasant.
> He'll sometime rise and go slashing, dashing, crashing off in seeming angry mood;
> He's depressed by age, as in bygone days, he has caused the town to flood . . .

Brazier's Yard, High Street. *London Borough of Havering Local Studies*

The worst known instance of flooding was to occur in 1888, when whole streets in the town remained under water for days. Just past the bridge, on the right-hand side, was the quaint weatherboarded facade of the Coach and Bell. Simmons may have dropped in to exchange greetings with the landlord James Seaward before continuing to its near neighbour, the Woolpack. Pressing on westwards down the High Street, Simmons would have noticed an increasing air of dilapidation. Brazier's Yard, also known as Ray Square, was a huddle of ancient buildings housing some of the town's poorest families. Simmons passed more tumbledown wooden houses on his left as he strode away from the town centre and High Street became London Road. Within a few minutes he had reached a district where, to the south, wooden barracks had housed up to six troops of cavalry during the Napoleonic Wars. Again, there was a steady stream of public houses: the New Mill, whose landlord in 1871 was 55-year-old cattle dealer John Rich; the Compasses, run by Joseph Finch; and the Sun, which dated from 1632.

The cavalry barracks had been demolished in 1825, and in the 1840s the site had been transformed by the erection of about 200 brick terraced houses, chiefly for working-class residents such as labourers at the brewery or the gas works. The district became known as New Romford, and its thoroughfares included Queen Street and St Andrew's Road (site of St Andrew's Church where, as we have seen, Simmons and Mary Ann had married in 1868). Running down the eastern side of the development was its major highway, Waterloo Road, whose inhabitants had a choice of two pubs, the Liberty Arms at the northern end and the Laurie Arms at the bottom, where it met St Andrew's Road.

If Simmons followed Waterloo Road southwards and under the railway line, it became Dog Lane, taking him into open country. Looking to his right at this point, he would have seen the looming shape of the huge Union Workhouse (later to become Oldchurch Hospital). It had opened in 1838 to house up to 500 wretched inmates from ten parishes, including Barking, Dagenham and Ilford to the west. The building inspired many local people with such dread that they went to great lengths to avoid travelling past it. Just to the west of the workhouse was a lane named Nursery Walk, after the plants and vegetables grown nearby. In September 1874 Simmons was patrolling in this area when he spotted a man carrying a sack which he tried to conceal in a hedge. The sack turned out to be full of turnips pulled up from nearby fields. The man, James Banks, had eight previous convictions, chiefly for similar thefts, and was sentenced to twenty-one days' hard labour.

Simmons would now be close to the spacious municipal cemetery, laid out in 1871 at the junction of Dagenham Road and Crow Lane. The land had been bought from 48-year-old farmer Ephraim Gray who, sadly, had a history of mental illness. Early on the morning of 27 October 1871, just a few days after the formal consecration of the cemetery by the Bishop of Rochester, Mr Gray's wife Eliza discovered his body hanging from a beam in the cart shed. She recalled: 'I think the selling of the ground for the cemetery seemed to prey upon his mind very much, and deranged him, as he has often said that he would never see anyone buried there.' John Archer, an employee of Mr Gray, had last seen him alive the previous evening, when 'he then appeared to be very merry'. Looking at the new cemetery, Mr Gray had sung 'O death where is thy sting, O grave where is thy victory?' If he had ambitions to be the first person buried there, he was to be disappointed. His body was interred in the old cemetery at Main Road, to the east of Laurie Town.

At other times Simmons would have been assigned a beat along North Street, which extended towards the villages of Collier Row and Havering-atte-Bower. When the streets were crowded he had to remember the Chief Constable's command in the *Orders and Instructions* manual to 'always to take the outward side of the footpath, and it is particularly desired that constables when walking along the streets should not shoulder past respectable people but give way in a mild manner'. Simmons would have checked that all was secure at St Edward's Vicarage on the western side of North Street, occupied in 1871 by the Reverend Edward Fox. Simmons may on some evenings have stopped off at the Roger Reede almshouses. In 1871 the inhabitants included 87-year-old former schoolmaster John Sloper, who would have had a fund of stories about the old coaching days. Mr Sloper had been born in Romford around 1784, which, coincidentally, was the year the almshouses were rebuilt. They had originally been founded in the fifteenth century.

A beat of a very different character took Simmons in the opposite direction from the town centre, down the increasingly rural Hornchurch Lane (the whole of South Street had formerly been known as Hornchurch Lane, but now that name applied only to the section south of the railway station). Ignoring Oldchurch Road, which branched off to his right about 300 yards from the station, Simmons would have walked for another five minutes up to the junction with Brentwood Road to his left. Here, at about 10.30 pm one evening in January 1873, Simmons met a horse and cart ambling along, seemingly with no driver. He climbed aboard and found a man named William Chandler fast asleep. Simmons, having been brought up in the countryside, knew that horses familiar with a route can be trusted to find their way home. He had no option, though, but to arrest Chandler for not having proper control of his vehicle, and a fine of 5 shillings was duly levied at the next Petty Sessions.

Leaving Brentwood Road behind, Simmons would stride along Hornchurch Lane until he reached the parish boundary with Hornchurch at Havering Well. This stretch being chiefly farmland, it comes as no surprise to find Simmons encountering poachers near this spot in the small hours of 30 November 1872. On hearing the tramp of feet he hid in a hedge, and soon saw two figures pass by, carrying nets and snares. He pounced on the men, Henry Philpott of Dagenham and Frederick Rayment of Romford, and they were subsequently charged with trespassing in search of game. Simmons may have found this area monotonous, with open fields on either side and few buildings. To historians, however, it was full of interest. They knew that the medieval chapel of St Andrew – the 'Old Church' of the place name – had been situated nearby, and it was thought that a settlement may have grown up on this spot long before the development of the present-day Romford lying to the north. A possible reason for the eventual decay and abandonment of the earlier settlement was its proximity to the River Rom, which, as we know, was prone to flooding.

At other times Simmons could not complain of lack of action. Romford traditionally had a reputation for unruly behaviour, especially at its annual one-day Midsummer Fair and at Guy Fawkes Night in November. Anti-police riots had occasionally occurred, but seem to have receded by the time Simmons arrived in the town. In 1880 local historian George Terry commented in his *Memories of Old Romford* that 'The practical and oft-times offensive jokes for which Romford was once notorious, belong to the past, except it be at election times'. The general election of February 1874, which saw Gladstone's Liberal Government ousted by the Conservatives under Benjamin Disraeli, must have tested Simmons and his colleagues to the utmost. Liberal supporters pasted yellow posters (this being their party's traditional colour) over the front of the Golden Lion in the High Street, and were only stopped when policemen managed to grab their paste buckets. More trouble occurred while electors were casting their votes at the neighbouring Corn Exchange. The *Chelmsford Chronicle* tells us that 'Certain of the assembly began to amuse themselves by throwing flour among the people, the consequence being that very many soon presented the appearance of millers; some few party fights also began to crop up between the rough element, and prudent shopkeepers in the vicinity of the polling booth soon put their shutters up.'

Thomas Simmons was promoted to constable 1st class on 1 May 1871, and now earned 23 shillings per week. Perhaps he and Mary Ann enjoyed some of Romford's range of leisure activities during his limited free time. The Corn Exchange, for example, hosted many types of concert. In March 1874 the Royal Poland Street

An early photograph of the eastern end of the High Street, with the Corn Exchange on the right. *London Borough of Havering Local Studies*

Temperance Handbell Ringers performed Handel's 'Harmonious Blacksmith', the 'Westminster Chimes' and many other items, ending with the audience joining the renditions of 'Let it Pass' and 'Scatter Seeds of Kindness'. A more glamorous occasion at the same venue was a Grand Ball in January 1873, with dancing to 'the inviting strains' of Messrs Coote & Tinney's Band.

Around the beginning of 1872 the Romford police said goodbye to Sergeant George Shead, and PC William Dennis was promoted in his place. On 9 September that same year came another change with the retirement of Inspector William Gilpin. He was replaced by James Pepper, who had been born in 1839 in South Weald, near Brentwood. Pepper had worked as a groom before joining the Essex police in December 1865. Five years later he had been promoted to sergeant 2nd class. In 1871 he was stationed at the force's headquarters at Springfield Court in Chelmsford, and his wife Sarah (née Coker) was housekeeper to the Deputy Chief Constable. Pepper was affable and popular, described as 'an active, cheery and intelligent officer, and a kind and genial neighbour'.

As we have seen, Romford's officers did not live at the police station, so ex-Inspector Gilpin remained at his former home in North Street while James Pepper settled in Eastern Road with his wife and small daughter. Their next-door neighbour was Charles Bamford, an auctioneer and estate agent who also held the post of deputy registrar of births, deaths and marriages. Charles's teenage son Alfred Bennett Bamford would later achieve fame as an artist, his output including countless watercolours and drawings of Romford and its surrounding areas.

On 18 December 1873 Thomas Simmons became a father again with the birth of his son William. The baby was baptized eleven days later at St Andrew's Church. This event was swiftly followed by his confrontation with the burglars in London Road, leading to the immediate arrest of one and the recovery of the stolen property. The items were valued at the considerable sum of £40. Simmons had followed to the letter the command in the *Orders and Instructions* manual stating that 'If after sunset, and before sunrising, the constable shall see anyone carrying a bundle, or goods which he suspects were stolen, he should stop and examine the person, and detain him.' The arrested man, in his early twenties, gave his name as John Smith but was soon identified as Samuel Golborne, of Blackwall. At the Chelmsford Assizes in March 1873 Golborne pleaded guilty to theft, and was sentenced to seven years' penal servitude. The trial judge, Sir Fitzroy Kelly, was full of praise for Simmons. Learning that a testimonial was about to be presented to the officer, Sir Fitzroy added £5 from court funds. The second burglar, Golborne's 19-year-old brother James, was captured soon afterwards. He pleaded not guilty, but was convicted by a jury. The judge handed down the same sentence as his brother had received, at which the unhappy prisoner yelled 'Strike me dead, rather!'

Superintendent William Bridges, of Brentwood, who had overall responsibility for policing Romford, had written to Chief Constable McHardy describing Simmons's actions. McHardy replied on 9 January 1874 that 'I wish you to raise the said constable to the Merit Class from the 1st inst acquainting him that his conduct is as creditable to himself as it is gratifying to me.' The merit class had been established three years previously, and was restricted to a maximum of ten sergeants and twenty constables. They wore a silver embroidered star emblem on each side of their collar, and also received a pay rise of a shilling a week (for constables) and two shillings a week (for sergeants).

From time to time Simmons and his wife had relatives to stay at their Victoria Road house. One such guest was Mary Ann's younger sister Ellen Jennings, born in 1848, who perhaps lent a welcome hand in looking after the two young children. At 2 Milton Cottages, two doors away from the Simmons family, lived a widow named Mary Ann Sexton and her son Alfred James Oxley, a clerk in the Ind Coope brewery. Simmons and Mary Ann must have been delighted to see romance blossom between Alfred Oxley and Ellen Jennings. The couple were married at Plumstead on 26 July 1875, and by 1881 were living in London Road, Romford, near the Slater's Arms pub.

In 1875 Thomas Simmons and his fellow officers had to accustom themselves to changes in the design of their uniforms. Helmets replaced the traditional top hats, and the frock-coats were traded in for shorter tunics. Two years later, on 1 November 1877, Simmons gained promotion to sergeant 2nd class. This ensured him a rise in pay to 33 shillings a week, including his Merit Class bonus. Sergeant Dennis remained in post at Romford, however, so it was necessary for Simmons to be redeployed after serving in the district for twelve years. He was sent to Epping, a market town some ten miles north of Romford, where he and the superintendent also had responsibility for the Sub-Divisions of Ongar and Harlow. Epping had formerly been renowned for its sausages, and like Romford it boasted a large number of pubs. In his 1888 *Dictionary of London*, Charles Dickens junior noted that 'About three in every four of the houses in the long straggling street of which it solely consists are inns'. Simmons was regarded as an expert in tackling cases of horse-stealing. This type of crime was widespread in the Epping area. According to John Woodgate, in his *Essex Police*, Epping was 'particularly favoured by thieves for the virtually unbroken cover afforded by the forest nearly all the way to London'. This may explain why Simmons was selected for the post there. He was further promoted to sergeant 1st class on 1 July 1878.

At some time before the summer of 1879 Simmons was transferred again, this time to Brentwood, six miles north-east of Romford. The town's police station in Queen's Road was, as we have seen, a Divisional Headquarters. Its Superintendent was John Dobson, born in County Kildare in Ireland. Dobson had joined the Essex Constabulary in 1865, the same year as Simmons, having previously served five and a half years in the Irish Constabulary. He had been appointed Superintendent at Brentwood in January 1876 on the promotion of William Bridges to the post of Deputy Chief Constable. Dobson was at that time unmarried, but was to wed Edith Maria Wallis, daughter of a Brentwood draper, in 1882.

An *Essex Times* report reveals that Simmons once more experienced the dangers of his work on 27 July 1879, when he was called to arrest a drunken labourer named Robert Goal, who had started a fight in a pub and was continuing the brawl in the High Street. Simmons managed to drag Goal to a cell at the police station, but the man then knocked him to the floor and set about him. Luckily Superintendent Dobson himself, only in his thirties and a strapping 5 feet 11 inches, was on hand to pull Goal away and overpower him.

Dobson later explained to the magistrates that, when drunk, Goal was 'about the worst fellow they had to deal with in Brentwood, but when sober he was a hard working, quiet and inoffensive man'. Although Thomas Simmons remained at Brentwood for a comparatively short time, the *Chelmsford Chronicle* noted that 'by his diligence and his quiet and courteous bearing, he gained the good will of all'.

3

'A Good and Valuable Officer'

In August 1880 the people of Romford heard that William Gilpin, their former police inspector, had died at the age of 73. Thomas Simmons probably attended at the Municipal Cemetery at Crow Lane when Gilpin was laid to rest alongside his wife, Ann Jane, who had passed away two years earlier. Four months later, on 28 December, came the shocking news that Gilpin's successor, 41-year-old James Pepper, was also dead. According to rumour, his fatal bout of bronchitis had been triggered by a night spent in a damp ditch watching out for a suspect. The *Essex Times* declared that Pepper 'lost his life through his strict and loyal devotion to duty'. A fund was set up to assist his wife Sarah and young daughters Florence and Violet. Frederick Wilson, the *Essex Times* proprietor and chairman of the fund committee's first meeting, praised Pepper as 'a man thoroughly reliable, and one whom nobody could help but liking'.

The funeral took place on 31 December, once again at the Crow Lane Cemetery. Thomas Simmons must surely have attended. Had he, perhaps, been in temporary charge at Romford during Pepper's illness? It seems likely for on 1 January 1881, the day after the funeral, it was announced that Simmons had been appointed as the new inspector of the Romford Sub-Division. It

An unidentified Essex Constabulary inspector, showing the uniform that Simmons would have worn.
Essex Police Museum

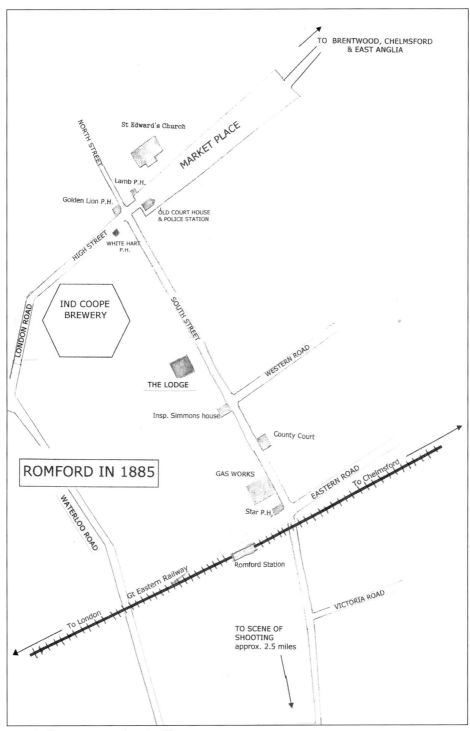

Romford in 1885. *Authors' collection*

was almost seven years to the day since his heroic encounter with the burglars in London Road.

Simmons was fitted for his inspector's uniform. The jacket was ornamented with black frogging, and the headgear was a képi, or stiff cap. Simmons would earn £90 per year as an inspector 2nd class, so he and Mary Ann could now afford something rather grander than their former home in Victoria Road. Their choice eventually fell on 56 South Street, one of a pair of semi-detached houses called Cavendish Villas. It had a small railed front garden and a long back garden, beyond which could be seen the sprawling buildings of the Ind Coope Brewery. Rate books show that the rent was £27 per annum, just over 10 shillings a week. The house was on the western side of South Street, opposite the junction with Western Road. Another pair of semis lay next to Cavendish Villas on their northern side, and beyond these there had been another two houses, which had been demolished in 1877 to make way for the building of the Congregational Church. On its southern side, the house was separated from the Romford Gas Works by a large field on which grazed the Ind Coope Brewery horses.

Fitting up Cavendish Villa to their taste, we can imagine Thomas and Mary Ann scouring the local shops for furniture and ornaments. Perhaps their gaze fell on the

South Street, Romford. The semi-detached Cavendish Villa, where Simmons and his family lived, is on the extreme left. The Congregational Church can be seen on the right. *London Borough of Havering Local Studies*

up-to-the-minute oven from John Pink's ironmongery store in the High Street. Mary Ann may have bought delicious cakes and pastries from William Muskett's shop at the corner of South Street and Eastern Road, ready for 'At Homes' at which she would entertain her new neighbours. One likely guest was 34-year-old doctor's wife Edith Wright. Ten years previously, Edith and her husband Alfred had lived at Laurie Square, but now they occupied The Lodge, the large house with its own carriage drive situated just a short distance to the north of Cavendish Villa. Edmund Vipan Ind, of the Brewery family, had lived at the Lodge until his death in 1871.

For Emily Simmons, aged 11, and her 7-year-old brother William, the move would have entailed a change of school. Romford's prominent tradesmen and other middle-class families sent their sons to the Regent House Academy, housed in an ancient building tucked behind the south side of the Market Place. According to legend, the cellar had been a hiding place for the notorious highwayman Dick Turpin. Their daughters were usually enrolled at the nearby Mrs Maria Clube's School for Young Ladies. The Simmons children, however, are more likely to have attended St Edward's National School, also in the Market Place, originally founded as a charity school back in 1711.

As we have seen, Simmons was responsible for the policing of the entire Liberty of Havering-atte-Bower, which had been established by a Royal Charter of 1465 and covered the parishes of Havering-atte-Bower, Romford and Hornchurch. It was, in essence, a manor owned by the Sovereign. Its inhabitants were granted special privileges, such as exemption from certain taxes and tolls and independence from the County of Essex in the administration of their own courts of Quarter Session and appointment of their own magistrates.

The high steward, or chief magistrate, according to the 1465 charter, had to be 'one of the "discreetest and honestest" tenants or inhabitants aforesaid, to be from time to time chosen by the tenants and inhabitants'. The high steward in 1881 could certainly be described as 'discreet' and 'honest'. He was Joseph Fry, eldest son of Elizabeth Fry, the great prison reformer. By trade a tea and coffee merchant, Mr Fry was now in his seventies. Following his mother's example, he was involved with many charitable organizations. He and his brother John Gurney Fry had founded the Metropolitan Free Hospital, which offered medical care to people 'whose only recommendations are poverty, destitution and disease'. He was also active in the Metropolitan Drinking Fountain and Cattle Trough Association. Mr Fry had lived since the late 1860s at Fairkytes in Billet Lane, Hornchurch. His wife Alice had died in September 1878, and there were eleven children of the marriage.

Mr Fry had formerly been deputy steward, and had been elected to the stewardship on the resignation of the Reverend Edward Fox. He had two deputy stewards. One was Ralph George Price, an oil merchant from Sydenham who lived at Marshalls Park, a spacious house situated off North Street. The other was Charles Peter Matthews, who occupied the Bower House in the village of Havering-atte-Bower. Matthews was a manager of Ind Coope, and followed in the footsteps of its founder, Edward Ind, who had once served as high steward of the Liberty. The pair were assisted by the clerk to the magistrates Henry Shekell Haynes, a solicitor born in Warwick who also held the offices of coroner to the Liberty and registrar of the County Court. In 1881 Henry Haynes was 37 and living with his wife Caroline and their children at Billet Cottage in Hornchurch, close to Mr Fry at Fairkytes.

Mr Fry seems to have been somewhat surprised at the appointment of Simmons as inspector. This was, after all, a man who had left Romford as a humble constable barely more than three years before. Fry was reported in the *Essex Times* as commenting that Simmons 'is well known to most of us . . . and from what we know of him, we have every reason to believe he will be a good and valuable officer; but it is almost unnecessary to say that he is not likely to equal the late Mr Pepper, who was a man out of ten thousand'.

Thomas Simmons was now responsible for a sergeant and fourteen constables. Some were men he had worked alongside as a raw recruit. One such was PC William Elms, now in his fifties, who had witnessed Simmons's wedding back in 1868. Elms was based at Collier Row, to the north of Romford, where he lived with his wife Sarah and numerous children. Elms retired on a pension 31 March 1882. He continued to live at Collier Row until his death aged 83 in 1909. The sergeant in post when Simmons became inspector was James Farrow, aged 42 and born in Epping. Farrow departed in November the following year, 1882, to be replaced by Simmons's old colleague George Samuel Chase. We have seen that Simmons and Chase had been sworn in to the force the very same day back in 1865, and subsequently posted to Romford together. In about 1870 Chase had been transferred to Terling, and from the mid-1870s had worked at Kelvedon. Chase had married Mary Dunn in 1865 and had a large family.

Simmons had only been in charge for six weeks when a storm blew up surrounding the recent arrival of the Salvation Army, who made their headquarters in North Street. Their journal the *War Cry* proclaimed that 'Captain Wood and Yorkshire Polly have been going up and down and around about the brewery-blighted town of Romford. They have invited the people who thirst to come and drink of the living water. Many have come, and others are

The Court House c.1900. In Simmons's time, the police station was on the ground floor.
London Borough of Havering Local Studies

coming, but the people generally are hard and unbelieving.' Matters came to a head on the evening of 16 February when singing Salvationists paraded through the busy Market Place. As they passed a crowd watching a Punch and Judy show outside the Lamb pub some pushing and shoving occurred, and Job Durrant, a carpenter, toppled to the ground. He claimed that John Wood, leader of the parade, had deliberately pushed him over. The case came before Mr Fry, who lamented that 'no man in the world can have a greater desire to see religion spread in every possible way than I have; but I cannot see that religion is promoted in this way'. He found Wood guilty of assault and fined him 20 shillings plus costs.

Thomas Simmons now, inevitably, found himself having to tackle administrative tasks. His job also encompassed the role of inspector of weights and measures, so he had to check the accuracy of weights used by the area's tradesmen. He worked alongside Thomas Pooley, the public analyst, in examining food and drink for possible adulteration. Simmons was also subjected to a stream of instructions from the magistrates at the Havering Liberty Quarter Sessions. In October 1882, for example, they called his attention to 'traction engines not being preceded by red flags as required by the Act, and the police be requested to insist on carts being properly protected'.

When Simmons took office as inspector changes were in progress in the area immediately surrounding the Court House. The building, as we have seen, stood at the western end of the Market Place on what seems to have been an ancient site. Behind its south side was a row of timbered buildings, thought to date from the fifteenth century, which had at one time made up the Three Crowns Inn. George Terry, writing in 1880, notes with regret that these ancient structures were then in the process of demolition. As for the Court House itself, by the time Simmons took charge it seems to have been decrepit and unfit for purpose. In October 1884 he suggested to the magistrates that 'the police office should be moved to the Jury Room upstairs and cells constructed in the present office, and the remaining cells reconstructed'.

Its four cells were damp and unheated, and so dilapidated that only two of them could be used. An additional problem was that the only public lavatory in the Market Place was a urinal attached to the outside wall of the Court House. It was prone to leaking, and the effluent seeped into the cells. Mrs Charlotte McIntosh, whose family had bought the manor from the Crown in 1828, was the lady of the

This group of Essex officers and their inspector (seated on the right) display the uniforms Simmons and his men would have worn in the early 1880s. *Essex Police Museum*

manor of Havering-atte-Bower and, therefore, the owner of the Market Place. The Romford Local Board negotiated unsuccessfully with her to build proper public conveniences. Simmons was also faced with a similar problem on the upper floor of the Court House. He reported to the Havering Quarter Sessions magistrates on 17 October 1883 that 'there is a leakage in the tank and I find there is frequently an offensive smell arising'. The same letter, preserved in the Essex Record Office, describes yet another problem with the building. 'On the 4th of October the iron chimney leading from the fireplace in the Police Station was damaged by the wind and it was so badly damaged that I was oblidged[sic] to have it taken down to prevent an accident to persons passing on the pavement.'

Simmons did not allow himself to be confined to desk duties, however. Tackling crime was meat and drink to him, as the *Chelmsford Chronicle* was to appreciate: 'The knowledge he possessed of the criminal class, with his undoubted intelligence, often enabled him to follow up clues with success, and he had assisted in breaking up and bringing to justice more than one party of thieves.' An example of this occurred in May 1881. William Ernest Drake had left a horse and cart in a lane near Collier Row, and on returning saw that the black overcoat he had left on the seat was missing. Simmons happened to be nearby, at Pettits Farm, and joined the hunt for the thief. He spotted a figure wearing an identical coat run along a lane and dive into a hedge. PC George Emery and local magistrate Mr Thomas Mashiter passed the place where the man was hidden. Simmons, however, was able to arrest the man, William Johnson, and ensure he was soon under lock and key at the police station.

Three months later, in August 1881, Simmons was called to Brook Cottage, off North Street, which had been broken into with the loss of a silver spoon and a box of sardines. He saw that the intruder had forced the kitchen door. Simmons returned to the police station to find that PC Emery had arrested a man named Richard Wiffen who had sold the stolen spoon and sardines to the landlady of the Windmill and Bells in the Market Place. Simmons went to the cell where Wiffen had been placed, and asked him to stand up and turn round. As Simmons had expected, the back of the man's jacket was covered with whitewash. The inspector had deduced that 'It would be impossible to force the kitchen door of Brook Cottage without coming into contact with whitening on the wall', and another successful prosecution followed.

At 10 pm on a cold night in October 1881 Arthur Sapsford, a boot maker, came across an abandoned 8-month-old girl, fortunately unharmed, lying in a lane north of Romford between Collier Row and Brooklands. Simmons circulated a description of the child and her clothing, and interviewed anyone who reported having recently seen her. Eventually the trail led him to Stradbrooke in Suffolk, where he arrested a couple named Mary Ann Chinnery and William Elvish who admitted abandoning the little girl.

In October 1883 a Miss Beckwith, manager of a coffee shop in the High Street, called the police when a woman paid for a bottle of ginger beer with a gold sovereign that appeared to be fake. Simmons confirmed that the coin was indeed counterfeit, and had been cleverly fashioned from a Hanoverian medal. He called upon Emma Archer, the wife of PC Charles Golding Archer, to search the suspect, and three more of the fake sovereigns were found on her. Giving her name as Kate O'Riley, she pleaded guilty and was sentenced by the Romford magistrates to three months' hard labour.

In September 1883 Simmons was called upon to investigate a case of serial shoplifting. A draper named Mr Wallis gave chase after spotting a woman stealing calico. He caught her and summoned the police. She was identified as Mrs Elizabeth Eary, wife of a brewer's labourer. Simmons and PC Frederick Day then frogmarched the culprit to her house in St Andrew's Road, and were astonished to discover a hoard of stolen goods from almost every draper's store in town, some still with price tickets attached. Apart from yet more goods belonging to Mr Wallis there were towels from Frederick Westgate's shop, a quilt from Denny Stone's store, and calico from William Taylor. Simmons reported to the magistrates that Mrs Eary said 'the reason she took the things was the small amount of money her husband allowed her'.

An exciting episode occurred in February 1882 when Henry Fox, landlord of the White Hart in the High Street, told the police that two guests named Amelia Maria Jackson and Caroline Rebecca Flack had returned from a church service to discover jewellery missing from their rooms. The chief suspects were Walter Smith and William Hills, who had vanished that very morning without paying their bill. Inspector Simmons couldn't resist joining the manhunt, accompanied by the White Hart boy-of-all-work, a lad named Dennis. In South Street Dennis pointed out Smith, who when confronted muttered 'I don't know anything about it, my friend paid the bill.' Not long afterwards Dennis spotted Hills in Victoria Road. When Simmons pounced, Hills admitted having the stolen jewellery. Simmons took the hat from Hills's head and made the wide-eyed lad Dennis hold it as a receptacle for the glittering objects that were soon being pulled from the man's pockets: six brooches, two lockets, spoons, gold and silver pencil cases, gold and silver crosses, gold rings, earrings, and gold chains.

Smith and Hills were put in a cell at the police station. Simmons, his ear to the door, heard Hills ask 'What did you do with your stuff?' Smith replied 'I threw it

The White Hart, High Street, scene of the jewel robbery foiled by Simmons in 1882.
London Borough of Havering Local Studies

away down the water closet. I heard one of the old women go up to the room.'
Simmons and his trusty juvenile sidekick Dennis (who must have told the tale
many times during his life) headed back to the White Hart, rolled up their sleeves
and got to work sifting through the contents of the sewage pipes. It was a case of
where there was muck there was gold and silver. The treasure included a silver
watch, a gold guard (a chain to attach the watch to a waistcoat), a gold seal, silver
fruit knife and pickle fork.

Simmons found himself in the thick of further dramatic events during his time
as inspector. Just before I am on Easter Sunday 1883 he and PC Stephen Peters,
having seen off a London-bound train, were walking down the slope from the
platform towards South Street. Suddenly a bright light caught Simmons's eye from
the direction of the Congregational Church about 100 yards away. 'The chapel's
on fire!' he yelled. The *Essex Times* reported that 'In a few moments the window

through which the fire had first been seen was blown out into the roadway, owing to the excessive heat, and from that time the flames, leaping over the archway at the back of the pulpit, spread with alarming rapidity.' The Ind Coope Brewery Fire Brigade was on the scene within fifteen minutes, but the whole church was soon burned to the ground, with the exception of the vestry. Astonishingly, it was rebuilt in just eight months.[5]

Just after 9.15 am on 22 April 1884, Simmons was alone eating breakfast when he suddenly heard a rumbling noise and felt his chair move. Thinking his wife was dragging a bed about upstairs, he went to the foot of the stairs and called up 'Why all that noise?' Meanwhile, at the police station, Sergeant Chase had been sitting at his desk writing a report when he was suddenly tipped from his stool, and several constables fell over. On picking themselves up they all ran outside, believing an explosion had taken place. The cause was, in fact, an earthquake centred near Colchester. Tremors were widely felt in Essex and beyond, and thousands of buildings damaged.

In October 1883 work began on the London, Tilbury & Southend Railway's new line from Barking to Pitsea, stopping at Dagenham, Hornchurch and Upminster. Liaising with the railway police, Simmons would have had to deal with public concern at the presence of hundreds of navvies working round the clock, seven days a week, some digging soil and loading it into trucks, which others shunted and unloaded.

In 1884 Simmons helped investigate a shocking case of suspected murder. William Harris, a soldier from Warley Barracks, spent the evening of Monday 19 May drinking with a Romford woman named Sarah Gilbert in Brentwood. The pair then took the 10.47 pm train towards London. The guard saw them enter a third-class carriage together, and noticed Harris get out alone at Harold Wood. On looking into the carriage, he found it empty. The guard challenged Harris, who immediately made his escape by jumping over a wall. Railway staff walked back along the line and found the unconscious and bleeding figure of Sarah Gilbert lying by the rails. She was carefully lifted into a train and taken back to Brentwood, but died soon after arriving at the railway station. Superintendent Dobson at Brentwood was able to communicate with Romford Police Station using the electric telegraph, which sent messages by wire. On learning what had happened, Simmons dispatched men to join the manhunt for William Harris and then travelled to Brentwood to help Dobson coordinate the search. The fugitive soldier was spotted later that evening by PC Galley near the entrance gates to the mansion of Dagnams, only half a mile from where he had got off the train at Harold Wood Station. Galley, noticing blood on the man's face and clothes, took him to Brentwood Police Station. It fell to Simmons to interview Harris and formally charge him with murder. Coincidentally, almost twenty years before, the very first arrest of Simmons's career had been of a man charged with indecently assaulting the very same woman, Sarah Gilbert.

In October 1884 a new pay scale was introduced. Having served less than five years as an inspector, Simmons would earn £95 per annum. He must sometimes have felt it small compensation for the stress of trying to maintain the service amidst a high turnover of staff. Six of his fourteen constables had left within the space of a year. One had resigned, another was dismissed, one promoted to sergeant and redeployed, and the remaining three had been sent elsewhere. In early January 1885 the Romford magistrates complained to the Chief Constable that with so many new officers unfamiliar with the area, 'they consider it impossible that the property of the inhabitants can be sufficiently guarded'. They added that 'Inspector Simmons has done his duty very efficiently during the time he has been in the Liberty notwithstanding the disadvantages he has had to contend with from the above cause . . .'

A light-hearted episode in October 1884, recounted in the *Essex Times*, must have afforded Simmons some relief from these strains. When a man burst into the police station claiming his watch had been stolen, Simmons sent officers to check at pawnshops and sellers of second-hand jewellery, but without result. The man said that some time previously a local watchmaker had repaired the watch, so Simmons advised him to go and ask whether its serial number had been recorded. The man did so, only to be told by the mystified watchmaker 'Do you mean the watch you left with me two hours ago to be repaired?' The embarrassed customer begged the watchmaker to let the police know what had happened, saying he 'never could go himself, they would think him such a fool!' He wrote a letter of apology to Simmons, which was 'retained as a record of one of the most extraordinary charges ever preferred at a police station, as well as a testimony as to how far it is possible for a man's memory to leave him'.

Two months later, in December 1884, Simmons investigated an alleged fraud by a cattle dealer. His talent in solving cases of livestock theft was once again called upon, and he was able to report to the magistrates that he had succeeded in tracing the whereabouts of the disputed cows.

On 22 December 1884 Simmons celebrated his fortieth birthday. Though in Victorian terms he would be considered middle aged, he was to be described in the *Pall Mall Gazette* as 'a fine-built, powerful man' and 'of splendid physique'. A few months previously he had suffered an unspecified illness, and undergone a painful operation, but had now regained his full health. With the coming of the New Year, Simmons and his 11-year-old son William would no doubt have eagerly followed the progress of Romford Football Club to the dizzy heights of the fourth round of the FA Cup, where they lost 4-0 to the holders, Blackburn Rovers. Mrs Simmons and Emily, now 16, may have been more interested in a flurry of royal events occurring at that time. At the close of 1884 Princess Beatrice, Queen Victoria's youngest child, became engaged to Prince Henry of Battenberg, and 8 January 1885 saw the twenty-first birthday of Prince Albert Victor, eldest son of the Prince of Wales. Reading about the birthday festivities at Sandringham, including a performance by Sanger's Circus, how could the Simmons family know that they themselves would soon be hitting the headlines?

4

'I am Done for This Time'

At about 3.15 pm on the afternoon of Tuesday, 20 January 1885, Thomas Simmons stepped out of Romford Police Station to go on routine patrol. With him was a young constable named Alfred Marden. The latter had just turned 22, having been born 4 January 1863 at Writtle, in Essex, the son of Reuben Marden, a hay binder, and his wife Eliza, formerly Reeve. Marden had worked as a groom before joining the Essex Constabulary in March 1883. That afternoon, the two officers climbed into their trap, drawn by a distinctive white horse. Marden was in civilian clothes, but Simmons wore his uniform and cap, plus a long overcoat against the chilly winter air. The temperature was below average for the time of year, and the morning fog had been replaced by a lowering gloom.

About forty-five minutes later, shortly before 4 pm, a man in his thirties named Frederick Wilderspin could be seen pacing the platform of the railway station at Rainham, a village about five miles south of Romford, a dog on a chain padding along beside him. Originally from Swavesey in Cambridgeshire, Wilderspin was a police constable at Dagenham, which fell within the jurisdiction of the K Division of the Metropolitan Police. He had married Susannah Goddard at the local parish church in 1882, and was now the father of a baby daughter, Ettie. Wilderspin, who was not in uniform, had travelled the three miles from Dagenham to Rainham that afternoon in order to put the dog on a train to London. No doubt he looked forward to the time, just a few months hence, when Dagenham would have a railway station of its own.

The four o'clock service from London arrived. It was terminating here. Nine or ten people got out, including three men who stepped from a middle carriage. Wilderspin's dog was a valuable breed, and caught the attention of the trio as they walked past him towards the ticket collector's booth at the end of the platform. 'They were undoubtedly in each other's company', the policeman later recalled. 'They looked hard at me and I took notice of them.' Wilderspin ensured that the dog was safely stowed away in the guard's van, then waited for the train to leave. After a ten-minute wait, the whistle blew and the locomotive steamed back towards London.

Meanwhile, Simmons and Marden had so far enjoyed an uneventful afternoon. While Wilderspin waited for the train, their horse and trap had been heading south along the lanes from Hornchurch. At a crossroads where the Cherry Tree pub offered refreshment they had taken the lower road towards Rainham. Around 4.10 pm, as Wilderspin was exiting Rainham Station, Simmons and Marden had passed Dovers Farm and were approaching the junction with New Road, which led away to Dagenham. Three men suddenly came into view walking towards them. As the horse and trap slowed to pass the pedestrians in the narrow hedge-lined lane, Simmons and Marden examined their faces.

The figures were strangers to Marden, but Simmons recognized one, in the words of *The Times*, as 'a desperate character and a returned convict'. This was 52-year-old David Dredge, who back in 1870 had been sentenced to seven years' penal servitude for horse-stealing. His lengthy list of other crimes included the spectacular feat of stealing a bell from a local church tower. Born at Hornchurch, Dredge was now known to be living in the East End of London. The presence of Dredge and his companions troubled Simmons. One was wearing what the *Essex Weekly News* described as 'the long "swag" overcoat generally adopted by those of the burglarious profession'. Simmons drove the trap round the next corner, then brought it to a halt out of sight of the men. He told Marden to get out and follow them on foot while he carried on to seek out PC Frederick Stock, the Rainham village constable.

When Marden came up to within thirty yards of the group, Dredge turned round and stared at him, then hurried to rejoin his companions. Marden strolled behind, keeping his distance. PC George Emery, one of the Hornchurch constables, appeared walking towards them, and Dredge greeted him with 'Good afternoon, sir'. When Emery reached Marden he told him the men seemed 'funny-looking characters'. Marden asked Emery to wait for Simmons while he continued to follow the group. It was now about 4.20 pm.

Meanwhile, Thomas Simmons had driven to Rainham and the neighbouring village of Wennington but failed to find PC Stock. He did, however, meet Frederick Wilderspin, who told him about the trio he had observed leaving the train. Simmons realized that their descriptions fitted the figures he had passed on the road. He bade farewell to Wilderspin, and was soon driving back the way he had come. On reaching the Cherry Tree junction he turned right into South End Road, and less than half a mile further on spotted Marden and Emery. Emery had waited fruitlessly for Simmons for some time before deciding to go on. He had caught up with Marden in South End Road near the junction with Ford Lane, and the pair had then stopped, having lost sight of the three men.

Simmons ordered Emery to take South End Road to Hornchurch, fetch his colleague PC George Selby Lowe and then 'work round the Hornchurch roads'. He

View of Bretons House as seen from the Rainham Road. *London Borough of Havering Local Studies*

and Marden then set off in the horse and trap down Ford Lane. On their left they passed Ford Lodge, home of Miss Louisa Tyler, who had died at the grand age of 90 on Christmas Day 1884, less than a month previously. At the junction with Rainham Road, Simmons turned right and continued northwards towards Romford for about a mile. Dusk was falling. Shortly before the point where the railway line currently being constructed from Dagenham crossed the road, a large eighteenth-century house named Bretons came into view on the left. Simmons and Marden were now two and a half miles from Romford Railway Station and the same distance from Rainham. Suddenly they spotted the men they had been pursuing. Marden recalled that 'they were about one hundred yards in front of us. They turned round and looked at us.' David Dredge then leapt through a gap in the hedge to his right into a field. His companions sprinted down the road.

Since 1869 the Bretons estate had been used by the Romford Board of Health as a sewage farm. Piped waste from the town flowed into two large tanks to be distributed as fertilizer over the 118 acre farm.[6] Three men named Edward Matthews, David Kemp and John (or Joseph) Sawkins had the unenviable job of working there as labourers. About 5.10 pm on that cold, dismal Tuesday evening they had put away their tools and set off in search of the warmth of their firesides, blissfully unaware that they were about to become entangled in an incident that would send a brief flash of high drama through their wearisome lives.

Matthews, a Suffolk-born widower in his thirties who lived in Queen Street,

Romford, later related that as he walked across the field towards the road he had seen two men standing by the gate from which a track led to the sewage farm. The taller figure was wearing an overcoat and a white wrapper. At the same moment the labourers became aware of the sound of a horse and trap coming along at some speed from the direction of Rainham, and recognized Inspector Simmons as the driver. Just before it reached the entrance to the sewage farm, the vehicle halted.

Simmons ordered Marden to leave the cart and go after Dredge. The constable got down and entered the field. Dredge was about six or eight yards ahead of him. Marden recalled: 'I said "What are you doing here, David Dredge?" and he replied "You bastard! I'll blow your bloody brains out with this", pointing his revolver at me.' Meanwhile, Simmons had urged the horse on sixty yards or so, where he caught up with the two other men and jumped down to where they stood at the right-hand side of the road. Marden later related that, still held at gunpoint in the field, he suddenly 'heard a report of firearms in the road in the direction the Inspector had taken. I turned my head and saw the tall man with a revolver in his hand, pointing towards the Inspector. I could see this through the gate openings and I also saw the smoke leaving the revolver.'

Edward Matthews, standing in the road, witnessed the unfolding drama. Simmons had demanded 'Show me what you've got about you!' and grabbed the

A contemporary depiction of the shooting of Simmons. *Illustrated Police News*

taller man by the collar. They struggled, and the man, whose back was turned to Matthews, tried unsuccessfully to get away. He then cried 'There you are, that's what I've got about me!' followed by an explosion and bright flash. Matthews recalled that 'At the moment that he shot they had hold of each other. I am quite sure about that. I should think that when the man fired the pistol must have been touching the Inspector's coat.' He didn't see the gunman pull out the pistol, so it must have already been in his hand. Matthews's fellow-labourer David Kemp reported that Simmons 'collared one of the men. Immediately afterwards something went bang! . . . The Inspector had previously collared the big man. I didn't see the pistol but I could see the fire plain enough.'

Simmons staggered backwards, shouting 'Stop him, I am shot!' The two strangers bolted back along the road to the gate leading to the sewage farm. The taller one hesitated, leaning on the gate-post, but his confederate urged him, with an oath, 'Go on!' They slipped through a gap at the side of the gate and made off across the grounds of the farm in the direction of Dagenham village, which lay about a mile to the west. On hearing Simmons cry out, Marden turned away from Dredge and sprinted towards his stricken comrade. 'He had not fallen, although he was staggering. I caught hold of him and leaned him on the cart. I asked him whether he could stand there. He said "Yes . . . the tall man done it"'. His clothes just below the waistcoat were wet with blood. Simmons urged Marden to leave him and pursue the men.

The constable courageously started across the fields. In the fading light he could just make out the shapes of the fleeing figures ahead of him. He yelled to the labourers 'Stop them, stop them!' Matthews and Sawkins joined in the chase, bravely pursuing the men in the full knowledge that they were armed. David

The culprits fleeing past the sewage farm gate. *Illustrated Police News*

Kemp, who was in his sixties, stayed behind. 'My mate ran on but I could not run, and the Inspector came and asked me to hold the horse.' About a hundred yards from the gate the tall man, presumably to facilitate his movements, threw off his long overcoat. Marden picked it up, roughly checked the pockets, then dropped it and resumed the pursuit. Newspapers described him as 'an expert runner', and he gradually gained ground. About a quarter of a mile from the dropped coat, some haystacks loomed into view. The fugitives ran between two stacks standing to their left. Marden headed for a gap on the right, but to his horror the men came round the corner running straight at him, both now brandishing revolvers. Marden saw the tall man fire, and as he twisted to avoid the shot his feet caught in the mud. As he fell, he was aware of the bullet passing over the right side of his face. He lay stunned for a few moments, not knowing whether more shots were fired.

Marden got to his feet and took up the pursuit once more. The men headed towards the River Rom, the boundary with the parish of Dagenham.[7] Marden recalled that:

> I was close behind them and they stopped and said if I went any nearer to them they would blow my bloody guts out. I think it was the tall man who said that. They crossed the river into some reeds and rushes into the next meadow. The river there is very narrow. I jumped over after them, but as it was getting very dark I lost sight of them.

Marden gave up the chase and turned back. He was surprised to see Simmons not

Marden gives chase. *Illustrated Police News*

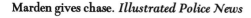

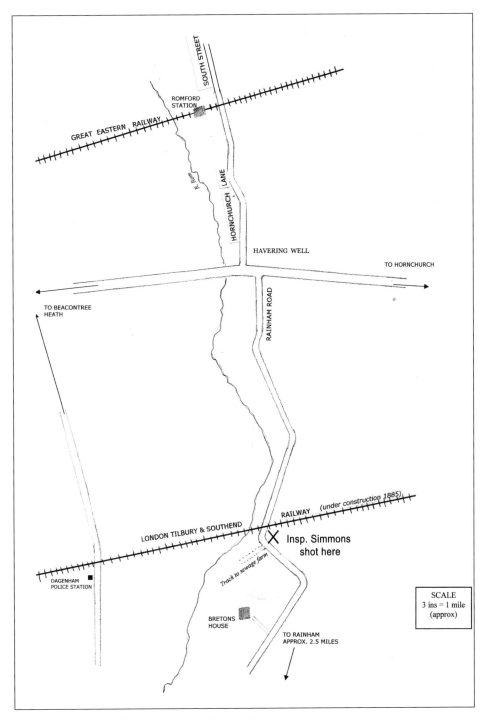

SOUTH STREET

ROMFORD STATION

GREAT EASTERN RAILWAY

R. Rom

HORNCHURCH LANE

HAVERING WELL

TO HORNCHURCH

TO BEACONTREE HEATH

RAINHAM ROAD

RAILWAY *(under construction 1885)*

LONDON TILBURY & SOUTHEND

✗ Insp. Simmons shot here

Track to sewage farm

DAGENHAM POLICE STATION

SCALE
3 ins = 1 mile
(approx)

BRETONS HOUSE

TO RAINHAM APPROX. 2.5 MILES

Map of the scene of the shooting. *Authors' collection*

far behind, leaning over a rail. His trousers were saturated with blood and he could hardly stand. Simmons gasped 'I think I am done for this time', took hold of Marden's arm and pleaded 'Don't leave me any more.'

Marden, Matthews and Sawkins could between them have carried Simmons back to his horse and trap, but the injured man himself had other plans. He ordered Matthews and Sawkins to return to the vehicle and take it to Romford Police Station. Marden and himself were to make their way to Dagenham Police Station, about two-thirds of a mile to the west. The inspector was evidently determined to alert the Dagenham force immediately so that the pursuit could be continued. Marden had no choice but to agree. He told the labourers to look out for the tall man's discarded coat and take it with them to Romford, as it might well provide valuable evidence.

Marden then set off with Simmons on a path across the fields, in the direction taken by the gunmen. As they stumbled along, Simmons rapidly lost strength. Marden recalled that 'He was very weak, and I had to stop on the road several times to rest him.' With some distance still to go, Simmons lost consciousness and dropped to the ground. Marden called out for help. His cries were answered by Mr Windmill, the engineer in charge of the sewage farm, who rushed to the scene with some labourers. They tried unsuccessfully to revive Simmons with brandy and other stimulants. Windmill then fetched a spring cart and Simmons was gently raised into it and driven across the fields towards Dagenham. The cart was filled with hay to make the journey more comfortable for the wounded man.

At about 5.30 pm Windmill halted the cart outside Dagenham Police Station, and Marden went inside to break the shocking news. Dagenham's 42-year-old inspector, John Durley, quickly took charge of the situation. Having telegraphed

Dagenham Police Station, where Simmons was taken after the shooting. *London Borough of Barking & Dagenham Archives at Valence House Museum*

Superintendent Dobson at Brentwood, he sent out armed officers to scour the immediate area, and dispatched a man on horseback to carry word to the neighbouring stations of Chadwell Heath and Barking. Unfortunately, Dagenham's medical man was not at home. Marden was soon back into the cart for the final leg of the journey, through Eastbrookend, then Rush Green, and finally into Romford itself.

As we have seen, when the wounded Thomas Simmons stumbled away to try to catch up with Marden and the others, he had left his horse and trap in the care of the elderly labourer David Kemp. The latter lived in Brazier's Yard, which, as previously mentioned, was a poor district just off Romford's High Street. His long working life had included a spell at the Ind Coope Brewery. Kemp's later statements allow us to piece together what happened next as he stood holding the animal's bridle.

About five minutes after the others had left on the chase across the fields, Kemp was startled by the appearance of a shadowy figure walking up the road towards him. Kemp saw that it was a man in his early fifties, quite well dressed in a dark overcoat and hard felt hat with a white neckerchief about his throat. Daylight was quickly fading and Kemp, whose eyesight may not have been as good as it once was, at first thought the man to be a stranger. After a brief exchange of words, however, he recognized the man as David Dredge, whom he had known by sight and formidable reputation for many years. This realization immediately instilled a sense of trepidation into poor Kemp. He jumped as Dredge addressed him sharply: 'Where are they gone?'

'They have gone across here', replied Kemp, nervously indicating the direction of the sewage farm. 'Them two men shot Mr Simmons. Didn't you hear the gun go off?'

'No', said Dredge. 'I shall stop here until they come back. I haven't done nothing. I shall stop to see what they want of me. I don't give a damn for old Simmons.' Dredge then told Kemp that he had been walking along with two men who had asked him to show them the way to Hornchurch. The minutes passed. 'I wish they would come back', complained Kemp. 'I'm cold and want to go home.'

'I'll look after the horse. You go on,' suggested Dredge.

'No!' retorted Kemp in alarm, knowing that he would be blamed if he gave this known horse-stealer such an opportunity. 'As I have stopped so long I will stop till they do come back.'

'Just as you like then,' Dredge replied with an air of nonchalance. 'I shan't wait any longer, I'll be on my way. Goodnight.' And with that, he walked away in the direction of Romford, having remained with Kemp about a quarter of an hour.

After what seemed like an eternity, Kemp at last saw Sawkins and Matthews appear, carrying the gunman's overcoat. Matthews took the reins of the cart and drove smartly off in the direction that Dredge had taken, but there was to be no further sign of him that night. At about 6.20 pm Sergeant Chase heard the inspector's trap draw up outside Romford Police Station. To his astonishment, the man who climbed down and rushed through the door was not Simmons or Marden but Ned Matthews. According to the *Essex Weekly News*, 'The fellow appeared in trepidation and excitement, and a collected account of the circumstances, or as to whether the Inspector was then alive or dead, could not be ascertained.'

On learning that the wounded Simmons was to be brought back in another vehicle, Chase sent two constables to South Street to meet it on the way. He quickly dispatched a telegram to Superintendent Dobson at Brentwood, then set out himself. He had not got far before the cart came into view containing, to his horror, the unconscious and bleeding figure of Simmons, supported by Alfred Marden. On the approach to Romford, Marden must surely have dreaded the impending confrontation with the inspector's wife. At that moment Mary Ann Simmons would very likely have been preparing supper for her family and expecting Thomas's imminent arrival from work. If no message had reached her about the shooting, we can only imagine her shock as she opened the door of Cavendish Villa. Her husband was carried upstairs and eased into bed. Mary Ann sat down beside the blood-soaked figure. A long, harrowing vigil was about to begin.

Dr Alfred Wright, their near neighbour, arrived at about seven o'clock. On examining Simmons he found a circular wound, two and a half inches below and an inch and a half to the left of the navel. It had evidently been made by a small bullet, which had passed through the abdominal wall. Later that evening Simmons regained consciousness, but vomited blood intermittently. To Wright, and his partner Dr Murray Smith who had joined him in the sickroom, this indicated internal haemorrhage, as would have been expected from such an injury. They were reluctant to probe for the bullet for fear of accelerating the bleeding.

Back at the police station, Chase and PC Leonard Alliston listened intently to the details of the attack on Simmons. Attention turned immediately to the overcoat which the tall gunman had thrown off as he had made his escape. It was dark grey, had a velvet collar and bore no maker's name. The pockets, however, revealed some interesting items. In the outside left-hand pocket was, in the words of *The Times*, 'a silk mask such as is used by burglars and others on such expeditions, but, curiously enough, it had only one hole cut for an eye to look through'. There was also a skeleton key, and a sheet of folded brown paper, which burglars carried to protect themselves whilst breaking windows. The right-hand outside pocket contained a white handkerchief. In the left-hand breast pocket was a purse containing seven revolver ball cartridges and cartridge case, plus a smaller skeleton key. This pocket also contained a pair of spectacles in a case bearing the label of an optician named Salmon of Seymour Street, Euston Square, London.

Superintendent Dobson soon arrived from Brentwood in response to the telegrams, and sent officers out in different directions to begin gathering evidence. Having obtained permission from the doctors to enter the sickroom to obtain an official statement from Simmons, he went to the bedside, accompanied by Henry Haynes and legal clerk William Smith. Simmons, speaking with great difficulty, said 'I quite understand you are taking the words now of a dying man'. Haynes later recalled that 'I said I thought it was serious for him, but I didn't like to discourage him too much.' Unfortunately, the task was too much for the enfeebled and exhausted man. By midnight his deposition was still far from complete, and the process was abandoned. The following morning, however, Simmons indicated he was able to continue. Dobson and Haynes were now joined in the room by the Chief Constable of Essex, William Henry Poyntz (who had been appointed on the retirement of McHardy in 1881). Magistrate Charles Matthews was also present as Simmons somehow mustered sufficient strength to give his account of the events of the previous day. It is rare to have such an account from the actual victim in a murder case:

I am an Inspector of County Police, stationed at Romford for the service of the Liberty of Havering-atte-Bower. I was on duty, in uniform, about 4 pm yesterday, Tuesday 20th instant. Coming along the lower road towards Rainham I saw David Dredge, whom I knew well and two others, whom I suspected of being there for some felonious intent, walking along the road towards Hornchurch. I was with PC Marden. I told him to watch them while I went on to Rainham. I could not find PC Stock and I drove back quickly towards Hornchurch. I found PC Marden and PC Emery near Ford Lane but they had lost sight of the men. I told Emery to go to Hornchurch – I went in search with Marden. When we got to the sewage farm it was dark. I thought I saw someone get into the ditch; Marden got out of the cart to see.

I drove on and came up with two men on the right-hand side of the road. I pulled up and said, 'Where are you chaps going to?' They said 'Home' and I said 'Let me have a look at you' and I got out of the cart on the same side of the road as they were. When I was about six or eight yards off, I think one of them – a tall man, six feet or so, no whiskers, little moustache and, I think, a fresh or sallow complexion – turned quickly round with a revolver in his hand and fired at me, saying, 'Take that!' – I think the words were. I felt a blow in the abdomen and I staggered back but did not fall. The man was one of the same men I had seen on the road previously. I had observed him and also the other – who was short and had clipped whiskers. The tall man had a long overcoat on which he must have thrown off whilst being chased. The short man had a jacket.

After I was shot the men jumped over to the sewage farm. Marden came up and I left the cart and chased them with Marden across the farm nearly to Dagenham. One fired twice at Marden – I can't say which it was. Dredge ran into Vince's field. I don't think he was present when I was shot. I am aware that I am dangerously wounded and that it may end fatally. I am afraid that it will – and that I shall not recover.

Immediately after witnessing the statement, Dobson travelled to Scotland Yard and spoke to Metropolitan Police Commissioner Sir Edmund Henderson. He was promised every assistance by the London force, beginning the same day with the deployment of extra constables to watch for the suspects at railway stations in and around the capital. On his return to Romford, Dobson had placards made and distributed:

WANTED, AT ROMFORD, CHARGED WITH SHOOTING INSPECTOR SIMMONS AND FIRING AT CONSTABLE MARDEN, THREE MEN OF THE FOLLOWING DESCRIPTION:

No. 1: About six feet high, no whiskers, stout build, dressed in round hard-felt hat, long black coat which he threw off when pursued, of respectable appearance.

No. 2: About 5ft 7ins high, clean-shaved, dressed in round felt hat and short jacket.

No. 3: David Dredge, late of Romford, about 52 yrs of age, 5ft 8ins high, grey whiskers and moustache, fresh complexion, grey eyes, dressed in hard felt hat and dark coat.

It was widely thought that the assailants would be lying low somewhere in the East End, but the *Essex Weekly News* speculated that they may have headed for a 'well-known point near Mud Island' and taken a boat across the Thames into Kent, 'where a wide and poorly-populated district lies before them, with every advantage incidental to a good start'. Local people believed that the men had planned to raid Ford Lodge, in Ford Lane, home of the late Louisa Tyler, which was rumoured to contain 'a quantity of plate'.

Meanwhile, the condition of Thomas Simmons worsened during the day. He was

Dr Alfred Wright, who attended the wounded Simmons.
Essex in the Twentieth Century: Contemporary Biographies (Pikes New Century Series, 27; 1909)

occasionally delirious, and unable to take any nourishment beyond a little ice and champagne. On leaving the house at 5 pm Wright and Smith stopped to speak to waiting newspaper reporters. According to the *Daily News* they feared the onset of peritonitis, and 'entertain but little hope of the Inspector's recovery'.[8] In view of the seriousness of the injury, they had sought the assistance of Mr Sidney Jones, chief surgeon at London's St Thomas's Hospital, who arrived later that evening in response to their telegram. Jones probed the wound for some distance, but was unable to reach the bullet. He thought it had taken a slight upward, diagonal direction, and had lodged somewhere in the locality of the hip bone. Simmons refused to be given chloroform or anodyne, and 'bore the examination with heroic fortitude'.

The following morning, Thursday, 22 January, the Havering Petty Sessions was held, and naturally the attack on Simmons was the chief topic. The magistrates had discussed the question of a reward with the Chief Constable, and announced that they would be offering one of £50. The Justices of the County of Essex put forward £100, and this was later supplemented by a further £100 from the Beacontree Division, who met at Stratford. Further placards were now printed offering the £250, approximately seven years' wages for a farm worker, 'to any person who should give such information as might lead to the apprehension and conviction of one or all of the offenders'. Application for additional funds was also made to the Treasury, although it was known that the Home Office was totally against the offering of rewards.

Meanwhile, back at Cavendish Villa, Simmons remained in a stable condition throughout that day, Thursday. He was still conscious, and the haemorrhage had ceased, apart from an occasional slight discharge from the wound, into which a tube had been inserted. During the afternoon he was visited by the Reverend William Maunder Hitchcock, vicar of St Edward's Church, to whom he spoke 'in hopeful terms'. In the evening Sidney Jones returned, and was surprised to find his patient somewhat better than expected. He announced that he now believed the inspector's chance of recovery was decidedly more favourable than he had thought the previous evening. Simmons passed a good night and obtained some sleep. The *Chelmsford Chronicle* told its readers that on Friday morning he 'was calm and free from pain and had apparently so well held his ground that hope was revived'.

Alas, this hope was to prove illusory. At about midday on Friday those attending to Simmons noticed a sudden change for the worse in his condition. Sidney Jones paid another visit in the evening. He saw that his patient was deteriorating rapidly, and stated his belief that there was now no hope. Simmons's elderly parents, Thomas and Sarah, would have travelled down by rail from their home at Weeley Heath. It must have been a terrible ordeal for them, as well as for the sick man's children, 16-year-old Emily and 11-year-old William.

Soon after 11 pm on Friday William Smith, the legal clerk, arrived with Simmons's original deposition. Keen to ensure that the statement was legally watertight, Smith had brought with him a Justice of the Peace, Frederick Green, of Hainault Lodge, Hog Hill. Smith read over the deposition in the presence of Green and Dr Wright, and in a voice enfeebled by pain, Simmons added: 'My depositions having been read over to me, I again confirm them in all respects as far as I am able. I firmly believe I am going to die.' This was now a 'dying declaration', defined by Maureen Scollan in *Sworn to Serve*, her history of Essex policing, as 'a statement taken from an injured and dying person as to the circumstances of his death. For the statement to be acceptable as evidence in court, the person who made it has to believe he is dying.' Smith read out this supplement to Simmons, who answered 'It's quite right', and signed the paper. Frederick Green also added his signature. By this time it was five minutes to midnight. Simmons shook hands with William Smith, and bade him 'Goodbye'.

One person who had not appeared at the bedside so far was Alfred Marden. Both he and PC Emery had of course seen the suspects, and had been kept busy since the shooting visiting known criminal haunts with London detectives in the hope of identifying them. On Friday Simmons had twice asked to see his young colleague, and so Marden waited outside the sickroom for Green and Smith to leave before going in. The *Essex Standard* reported that 'Simmons seemed very pleased to see him, shook hands with him warmly, and after inquiry after his health, bade him "good-night" and dropped off to sleep.'

Marden remained until 8 am, accompanied for much of the time by Dobson, then left to make way for the Reverend Hitchcock to administer the Holy Sacrament to Simmons.

Marden returned shortly before 10 am, and as soon as Simmons saw him he suddenly roused himself and asked 'Marden, are you shot much?' Marden assured him that he had not been shot, and was completely uninjured.

'Are you sure of that?' queried Simmons. Marden replied 'Quite sure', to which Simmons smiled and turned his head. He dozed for a few minutes, then turned to Marden once more and asked 'Don't I owe you some money?' Marden assured him he did not.

'I know I am going to die shortly', said Simmons, 'and I am quite prepared for it. Bid good-bye to all the men for me, and tell them to be kind to poor Willie.' He then asked for Alfred Oxley, his brother-in-law, and whispered a few words to him, probably asking Oxley to do his best to look after Mary Ann and the children.

To the anguished watchers standing helpless at the bedside, it was evident that the end could not be long in coming. Simmons was calm and peaceful to the end and, though often seized with spasms of pain, spent his last hour in solemn prayer. His hands and feet grew cold, and at ten minutes past eleven on Saturday 24 January Simmons slipped peacefully away. The *Chelmsford Chronicle* reported that 'the sufferer ultimately died almost without a struggle. He was conscious up to the last moment.' Mary Ann Simmons was said to be 'prostrate with grief'.

5

'He Loved His Work Too Well'

The announcement of the death of Inspector Simmons cast a palpable mantle of gloom over Romford. The *Essex Times* of 28 January stated that 'in all our experience we remember no incident connected with the town which has so deeply stirred the feeling of all classes as has the atrocious crime committed in our midst last week'. It aroused at once a profound sympathy for Mrs Simmons and her children and deep-seated contempt for his killers. On Saturday afternoon and Sunday, Mary Ann was visited by members of many leading local families expressing their condolences.

Newspapers paid generous tributes. The *Chelmsford Chronicle* declared: 'The great exertions the Inspector made after being wounded to secure the men no doubt went far to extinguish whatever little chance there was for him . . . It was probably due to his fine constitution and his nerve power, which never gave way under the cruel strain, that his life was prolonged as long as it was.' The *Essex Times* was also full of praise for the murdered officer:

> Intelligent, and far-seeing in all matters appertaining to the work of the police, he was extraordinarily vigilant, ever to be found at his post, morning, noon and night . . . Whilst he courted no man's favour so he feared no man's frown; but having laid down for himself a strict line of duty, he pursued it unfalteringly, swerving neither to the right nor to the left as much as a hair's breadth. In a word he loved his work too well. Had he been less brave and had he cared less for the interests of the public he would still have been carrying out the duties of his office.

The *Essex Times* printed these poignant lines:

> How should a Hero die?
> On battle plain, with waving sword,
> And the wild onward rush and joy
> Of glorious victory?

How should a Hero die?
The soldier when he nobly falls,
His name inscribe on glory's roll,
His deeds in history?

How should a Hero die?
Noble deeds are often done
Unknown to fame, when duty calls
Crime to detect, defy!

How DID a Hero die?
On daily duty's battle plain,
By coward hand shot down and slain,
Who turn and fly.

THUS did a Hero die!!
Now the mourners' chaplet weave,
Give unto him for whom we grieve,
A Hero's immortality!

The *Globe and Traveller* was quick off the mark, printing the sad news in its afternoon edition the very day of Simmons's death. It reported that 'A photograph of the man Dredge has been obtained and his apprehension is hourly expected.' Also on that day the Essex police authorities announced that Alfred Marden had been promoted to merit class for his 'gallant and meritorious conduct at Hornchurch', gaining him a pay increase of a shilling a week. Marden's colleague Frederick Day received worse news. He was fined 10 shillings 'for being under the influence of drink and absent from duty at Romford at 10 pm on the 16th inst'.

At about 4 pm on Saturday 24 January, five hours after the death of Simmons, a labourer named Joseph Knight was cleaning a ditch on land farmed by Mr Gill near Dagenham village. Behind some bushes Knight spotted a key-hole saw, together with what was described by *The Times* as 'a pair of socks with felt over the soles, evidently used for the purpose of being drawn over the boots in order to deaden the sound'. PC James Coombs quickly arrived at Gill's farmyard in Bull Street to collect the items. The following day Dobson and Marden went with Knight to the site of his discovery. Marden judged that it was about 100 yards from the spot where he lost sight of the men, and lay in the direction the men were heading. The objects were taken to Romford Police Station and carefully lodged with the other pieces of evidence. It seemed that to avoid being caught in possession of tools of burglary, the men had resorted to the drastic action which had cost the inspector his life, then disposed of the incriminating items while making their escape.

The Times ran an editorial on Monday, 26 January using the Simmons case to initiate a debate about the current widespread availability of firearms. It stated that 'An epidemic of revolvers and the violences attendant on the habit of carrying them has been ravaging the United Kingdom', and reported that customers ordering made-to-measure coats often instructed tailors to add special pockets for holding revolvers. The *Graphic* of 17 January 1885 featured an advertisement for a G E Lewis, gunmaker of Birmingham, offering a 'Choice of 2000 guns, rifles and revolvers. Revolvers from 6s 6d to 100s.' The editorial of the *Essex Weekly News* of 23 January declared that 'The use of firearms by these desperadoes has been too frequent of late to be at all comfortable to the guardians of the peace, in whose trust the public place the safekeeping of their property, their homes and their lives.'

Another dramatic story now dominated the headlines. On the afternoon of the day that Simmons died, London suffered a major terrorist attack, part of an ongoing campaign by the Fenians, an Irish Republican organization.[9] Bombs exploded inside Westminster Hall, the House of Commons and the Tower of London, all open to the public at the time. There was widespread damage, but amazingly no lives were lost. Rumours spread of possible impending attacks on landmarks such as the National Gallery and the various Thames bridges. The attack followed an incident on the London Underground a few weeks earlier, on 2 January, when a bomb had been thrown from a westbound train shortly after leaving King's Cross Station. A passing train going the other way was severely damaged, but fortunately there had been no serious injuries. The Metropolitan Police Commissioner was allowed to increase the strength of his force by one inspector, five sergeants and 108 constables 'to replace officers withdrawn for special protection duty'.

Back in Romford, on Sunday 25 January Alfred Wright performed a post-mortem on the body of Thomas Simmons. He discovered that the bullet had passed transversely across the abdominal cavity, finally becoming embedded in the lowest bone of the spinal column. Its course had severely damaged the large intestine, bringing about the fatal onset of peritonitis. Wright removed the bullet, together with fragments of clothing carried in its course and embedded in the intestines. The bullet weighed two drachms (equal to a quarter of a Troy ounce under the apothecaries' weight system) and seemed identical to those found in the gunman's overcoat.

The following evening, Monday 26 January, Henry Shekell Haynes, in his capacity as coroner for the Liberty of Havering, opened the inquest at the County Court House in South Street. He began with a few words of tribute to Simmons.

> I am satisfied you will agree with me that the death of the Inspector will be a great and serious loss not only to this Liberty but also to the County Police . . . I have always found him straight forward, energetic, active, honest and truthful and I am well sure that no better man than he will be found to carry out the duties of the Inspectorship in this part of Essex.

The members of the jury, whose foreman was Sussex-born John Thomas Pink, a High Street ironmonger, nodded their heads in emphatic approval.[10] After being duly sworn, they were escorted across the road to Cavendish Villa to view the body.

Upon the jury's return, Alfred Marden was the first witness to give evidence. He described the suspects, stating that he had first had a good look at them from the horse and trap. 'The tall man who shot the Inspector', Marden declared, 'is about six feet high, dark hair, and his eyes are sunk in. He is rather a bony-made man . . . He was a little round-shouldered and he had no whiskers.' On being asked whether the man had a moustache, he replied 'I think not. If he had, it was very little.' The second man, according to Marden, 'was about five feet seven inches high . . . I didn't see so much of him as of the other. He had a moustache and whiskers, but had his skin shaved. He was inclined to be ginger.' Marden added that he formally identified the body. The coroner asked Marden to confirm that Simmons had been wearing uniform, explaining that 'the Legislature had made very special provision for the protection of constables and others when in the discharge of their duties, and the law in such cases implied malice and premeditation'.

Edward Matthews was the next called, and described how he had seen the inspector gunned down. When asked how close he had been to the men at the moment of the shooting, Matthews replied that he was 'rather more than the length of this room from them'. He then related how he had followed Marden in pursuit of the suspects. 'Did you find anybody in charge of the cart on your return?' asked the coroner. 'Yes,' replied Matthews, 'A man named David Kemp.' And so came Kemp's turn to face his ordeal in the witness box. Completely innocent of any criminal act, but fully aware of the depth of feeling against David Dredge, Kemp seems to have been determined to avoid even the slightest implication of any previous association with him. He described how a man had come up and spoken to him for about ten to fifteen minutes while he was minding the pony and trap. Haynes asked if there was anything more to add, and Kemp said there was not. He was about to step down when Superintendent Dobson informed the court that there was a serious omission in the witness's evidence. The *Essex Times* reported the exchanges, verging on the comical, which followed.

Haynes asked Kemp: 'Don't you know who the man was?'

'Yes,' admitted Kemp reluctantly, 'He said he was David Dredge.'

'When did he tell you that?'

'When he first came up to me. He said "Inspector Simmons called me David Dredge"'.

The jurors were becoming somewhat confused. One of them, Peter Reynolds, landlord of the Golden Lion, enquired, 'Did you know him as David Dredge or did he tell you so?'

'He told me so.'

The coroner demanded 'Did he come up to you and say "I am David Dredge?"'

'He said Mr Simmons came up to him and said to him "What are you doing David Dredge?" and Dredge told me that he had gone to the hedge for a necessary purpose.'

The jury had by now deduced that Kemp knew more than he was letting on. An intense volley of questioning was fired at the hapless old man, who became increasingly edgy as the interrogation proceeded.

James Patching wondered if he would know the man who came up and spoke to him. 'I have no doubt I should.'

'Did you know Dredge by sight when he came up to you?' pressed the coroner.

Eventually, Kemp was forced to admit 'Yes, I had seen him before, but it was a long time ago.'

'Didn't you know his name when he came up to you?'

'No, not until he came up to me. I had no suspicion of him; in fact he frightened me when he came up.'

'How long have you known him?' demanded Haynes.

'Fourteen or fifteen years ago. I have not seen him much since.'

'You mean by that you have since met with him now and then? Can you remember the last time you saw him before this night?'

'No.'

'Have you never had any dealings with him?'

'Never.'

'Did you know anything of him when he got into trouble about a horse?'

'I know the family got into trouble about a horse'.

'As soon as you saw his face, and entirely apart from his telling you his name, didn't you recognize him as David Dredge?'

'I will swear I did not.'

'Very well,' sighed Haynes, 'we will take your answer. But you will get yourself into trouble if you are not careful. This will go elsewhere.'

Failing to seize this opportunity to be let off the hook, the cantankerous Kemp pressed his point. 'I don't know what trouble I can get into. I am telling you all I know.'

'I warn you to be careful, sir!' seethed the coroner. 'You have already as nearly as possible perjured yourself and unless you are careful I shall give you time for reflection. Now then, do you mean to swear that there never have been any business dealings between you and Dredge?'

'No, never.'

'When you were sworn to tell the whole truth why didn't you commence your evidence by telling us that this man told you his name was David Dredge?'

'I did tell you so.'

'Nothing of the kind. I put the question to you, and you said "A man came up". You never mentioned a word about the man's name until I afterwards pointedly questioned you. You will swear that what you have told us is the whole of the conversation that took place between you and him whilst you were holding the horse?'

'Yes.'

'Didn't Dredge say where he had come from?'

'No. He said he had come with two men who had asked him the way to Hornchurch.'

'You never told us that before. Did he say what two men?'

'No.'

'Did he say the two men that ran across the field?'

'No.'

'Did he say where the men had gone? You know two men cannot disappear into the air.'

'No.'

And so it went on, question and answer, with Kemp adamantly refusing to drop his guard. The *Chelmsford Chronicle* summed him up as 'rather insolent and very evasive'. Eventually, Haynes was forced to concede: 'Do you mean to say that after you had been talking to him you did not know him as David Dredge whom you knew previously?' 'No, sir.' 'All I can say,' said the exasperated coroner, 'is that if you get into the Assize court I shall pity you. Very well, you may stand down.' With visible relief upon his face, Kemp scurried from the witness box.

When all evidence had been heard, there was a brief discussion between the members of the jury before their foreman, Mr Pink, announced: 'Our verdict is that of wilful murder by some person or persons unknown.'

Descriptions of the three fugitives were sent to the *Police Gazette*, repeating what Marden had told the inquest but adding that the first man was about 25 years of age and around 6 foot tall, and that David Dredge had grey eyes, 'long scar left eyebrow and extending across forehead, scar on left thumb, little finger has been broken'.

The following day, Tuesday 27 January, exactly a week after the shooting, the funeral of Thomas Simmons took place. The undertakers, Messrs J S Hammond & Son, had placed the body within a lead coffin enclosed by an outer one of polished oak. The cortege left the house at two o'clock, but well before this time people were gathering along the route despite the threatening prospect of the winter weather. The *Chelmsford Chronicle* commented that 'no demonstration on such a scale has been witnessed in Romford for many years'. All shops and businesses of the town were closed, and even the humblest dwelling had its blinds pulled down as a mark of the widespread respect felt for the late inspector.

The procession to the municipal cemetery at Crow Lane extended more than a quarter of a mile. It began with a long line of Romford and Brentwood residents

Major William Poyntz, the Chief Constable of Essex (left) and his deputy Raglan Somerset (right), who both attended the funeral of Simmons. *Essex Police Museum*

walking two abreast, followed by the glass-sided hearse of the type known as a Washington Car. The crowds of onlookers lining each side of the roadway craned their necks to see the coffin, covered with a vast array of floral tributes, including a handsome wreath from Sergeant Chase and the constables who had worked under Simmons at Romford. Immediately behind came the coach carrying the inspector's brothers Henry, Ralph and Charles, his brother-in-law Alfred Oxley and his son William. (It was not at that time customary for women to attend.)

There then followed the representatives of the Essex Constabulary led by the Chief Constable, Major William Poyntz, and his deputy Raglan Somerset. It was an impressive contingent of over a hundred officers marching four deep, their silver helmet badges covered with black crepe. Behind them came a similar delegation of about a hundred members of the K Division of the Metropolitan Police, as well as Inspector Foster of the Great Eastern Railway Company Police and his officers. There was also a committee representing the 'Sir Robert Peel' Court of the Ancient Order of Foresters, a friendly society of which Simmons had been a member since March 1868. There then followed the carriages of Messrs Fry, Matthews and Price, together with Mr Haynes and Mr Benjamin Baker of Brentwood.

The shortest route from Cavendish Villa to Crow Lane Cemetery would have been south past the railway station along Hornchurch Lane, then right into Oldchurch Road. It was decided, however, to take a much more roundabout route so that as many people as possible could see the procession. It travelled up South Street to the Golden Lion crossroads, where the hearse probably stopped for a while at the police station. The cortege then turned left into the High Street, left again into Waterloo Road, then under the railway bridge. Next it passed the workhouse, where its master, Henry Seymour-Clarke, with members of the board of guardians, joined the procession.

More mourners waited at the cemetery gates a short distance away, where the cortege was met by the Reverend Hitchcock. Over 2,000 people strained to hear him intone the solemn funeral service. Each side of the pathway was lined by police as six of Simmons's fellow Essex inspectors bore the coffin, first into the chapel and then to the spot where it was committed to its final resting place. Charles, the youngest of the three Simmons brothers present that afternoon, was so grief-stricken that it took much persuading before he would leave the graveside and get back inside the coach for the return journey. There was one final touch of poignancy. As the ceremony drew to its conclusion in the fading light of the winter's afternoon, the men of the police contingent were brought to attention. Then, as one, they turned smartly about and marched resolutely away towards the

The grave of Thomas Simmons in Crow Lane Cemetery.
Essex Police Museum

Market Place where they would finally disperse, the tramp of their boots growing ever fainter as they faded into the misty distance.

In the days following the funeral of Inspector Simmons a deep depression enshrouded not only the Simmons family, as was to be expected, but also the vast majority of the people of the town of Romford. As they tried to carry on with their day-to-day affairs, the plight of the widow and two young children was never far from their thoughts. In those days, before the advent of the Welfare State, a widow could, unless she had been well provided for or possessed wealth in her own right, find herself in very difficult circumstances, relying on the mercy of a notoriously cold charity. Such was the respect and admiration felt for the late inspector, however, that steps were quickly taken to alleviate any financial anxiety Mrs Simmons may have had. All that she could have expected to receive from the Essex police in compensation for the life of her husband was a lump sum payment equivalent to his pay for one year – about £90.

On Thursday 29 January, two days after the funeral, a meeting was convened at the Golden Lion with a view to setting up an appeal fund. It was attended by about twenty-five local businessmen and local government officials, and chaired by the Reverend Hitchcock. A committee was appointed to administer the fund. The inquest jury donated their fees, and pledges received that evening meant that the total already stood at £100. The *Essex Weekly News* reported that Superintendent Dobson handed in £5 from a resident of Brentwood, 'who never saw Inspector Simmons in his life, but who presented it owing to his strong feeling of admiration for his conduct'.

6

'One of the Cleverest Detectives in the East End'

The day Thomas Simmons was buried, there was drama when a stranger matching the description of one of the suspects was seen in the Essex village of Southminster. The *Chelmsford Chronicle* reported that 'Being unable to give a satisfactory account of himself, he was taken to Latchingdon in order that further inquiries might be instituted'. Alas, it soon proved to be a case of mistaken identity. Some newspapers were already criticizing the police over the lack of results so far. On Monday 26 January an editorial in the *Globe and Traveller* thundered:

> The man who shot the unfortunate Inspector Simmons is still at large, and the authorities are feebly groping after him by means of absurdly paltry rewards. Yet there seems no mystery whatever about the man. One of his companions was well known to both the policemen and he could not have got far away by the time the news reached the nearest police station. Why he was not caught at once is the real mystery.

The hunt for David Dredge intensified, but many wondered whether he would ever be captured alive. According to the *Police Guardian*, a rumour circulated on the afternoon of the funeral that Dredge had been shot by his accomplices. The *Essex Weekly News*, on the other hand, claimed that while waiting by the horse and cart Dredge vowed to kill himself rather than be arrested. He had then headed towards a nearby wood, and about five minutes later Kemp had heard two shots ring out from that direction. In response to this startling tale, Sergeant Chase and PC Emery thoroughly searched the wood. It was reported that they 'found traces, no doubt, of the fugitive Dredge, and a quantity of wood pigeon feathers, but no signs of a dead body'.

The notorious Dredge had been a thorn in the side of the Romford police for many years. He had been born in nearby Upminster on 23 March 1834, son of David and Amelia Dredge. His father was a thatcher and agricultural labourer who died aged only 35 when David junior was 13. There had also been two daughters – Eliza, three years younger than David, and Amelia, who had died at just one month old in January 1836. The widowed Amelia Dredge earned a scanty living by doing needlework, and young David would have left school at 12 or even earlier to work as an agricultural labourer.

On 23 December 1855 David, then 21, had married 17-year-old Mary Ann Aylett at St Edward's Church, Romford. His bride was a stepdaughter of John Holder, landlord of the Plough Inn at Gallows Corner, Romford Common.[11] Her own father John Aylett, a straw carter of Beacontree Heath in Dagenham, had died aged just 28 in 1842. By 1861 young Mr and Mrs Dredge were living at Chadwell Heath, where David had set himself up as a hay and straw dealer. His father-in-law John Holder died in 1866 aged 50. As well as being landlord of the Plough Holder had also run a hay and straw business from the premises. His widow Mary afterwards managed the pub, and it appears that Dredge moved from Chadwell Heath in order to take over the hay and straw dealing. Inspector Simmons had of course known the Plough well. In March 1873 he had charged Joseph Mays, its landlord at that time, with opening beyond the permitted hours.

David Dredge's long list of convictions, dating from 1860, included drunkenness, violence, wilful damage and assault on the police. The *Essex Times* tells us that a bell vanished from Childerditch Church but 'Ultimately however it was traced – so much of it at least as remained – to Dredge's Yard at Romford Common where it was found buried under a heap of dung.' Unsurprisingly, Dredge's business eventually collapsed and he had to take what work he could, even humble temporary agricultural jobs such as hay-binding. Dredge at one time received a serious head injury by falling from a wagon and striking its wheel. The result was that even the smallest quantity of alcohol would render him 'fighting-drunk', and sometimes it took several policemen to restrain him. In the *Essex Times* of 28 February 1885 a recent employer of Dredge described him as 'a firebrand', and went on:

> Dredge was always of a pugilistic turn of mind, and this love of fighting often led him into scrapes. So pugnacious was he that if an opponent was down, or disinclined to rise and renew operations, Dredge would so far accommodate himself to circumstances, as to offer to lay down beside his foe, and resume the melee under these equal but eccentric conditions.

Despite this, the employer had found no fault with the manner in which Dredge carried out his duties, and had often placed him in positions of trust which he had never abused.

The marriage of Dredge and Mary Ann was unhappy and childless. Dredge had at least one mistress, a Mrs Sarah Boram who lived at Anne Street in Poplar. In

November 1869 it was discovered that a horse in Dredge's stable had been stolen from a man named Stephen Barber at Little Ilford six months before. Horse-stealing traditionally attracted a heavy punishment, and at the Essex Assizes in January 1870 Dredge was sentenced to penal servitude for seven years. It was rumoured that his own wife Mary Ann, sick and tired of his abusive treatment, had tipped off the police and then taken ship for America.

After an initial spell under the 'separate system' at Pentonville, under which the inmates had contact only with the prison staff and chaplain, Dredge was transferred to Portland Convict Prison, Dorset. Here, back-breaking labour in the stone quarries, a meagre diet, and merciless discipline (enforced, where necessary, with the cat o'nine tails) were the order of the day. Prison records held at the National Archives reveal that, although Dredge occasionally got into trouble for such faults as idleness and losing his tools, he was eventually allowed a ticket of leave in July 1875. Three years later, on 14 July 1878, Dredge married Charlotte Eastall, daughter of bricklayer James Eastall. The ceremony took place at St James the Great in Bethnal Green, with Dredge describing himself on the register as a widower. At the time of the 1881 census Dredge, now a 'corn merchant forage foreman', was lodging at 46a Commercial Road. Mysteriously, he was listed as 'unmarried'.

So with the knowledge that Dredge had lately been living in the East End, the search for him was concentrated within the labyrinth of slum tenements and cheap lodging houses which lay east of the City of London. In spite of the growing amount of purpose-built housing for the working classes such as the Peabody

Convicts at work stone quarrying at Portland Prison, as depicted in the *Graphic*.
Authors' collection

Estates, hundreds of thousands of people were forced to eke out an existence in the squalor of crowded, crumbling, bug-infested tenements. While the majority accepted their lot and struggled bravely to scrape a living in their dire surroundings, there were inevitably some who, faced with penury and the workhouse, chose a life of crime. Police officers patrolling the East End were frequently issued with firearms, but there still remained areas into which they would enter only in pairs and then only during daylight.

Uniformed police were not the only ones hunting for Dredge. A Detective Branch of plain clothes officers had been set up in 1842, but was not universally welcomed. Many people had been somewhat sceptical of Robert Peel's 'New Police' from its founding in 1829, and its Detective Branch was subject to even more suspicion, being seen as reminiscent of the secret police of revolutionary France. A major trial of five senior detectives for corruption in 1877 led to a complete review and reorganization of the Detective Branch. The result was the establishment in 1878 of the Criminal Investigation Department, with headquarters at Scotland Yard and detectives allocated to all divisions of the Metropolitan Police around the capital.

One such officer was 37-year-old Detective Sergeant William Elias Rolfe, assigned to H Division, Whitechapel, one of the roughest, most violent and lawless districts in London. He had been born 23 July 1847 at Aldbourne, Wiltshire, the first child of George Rolfe, a boot and shoe maker, and his wife Elizabeth, formerly Pearce. The family later moved to Amesbury, also in Wiltshire, and after George Rolfe died in 1852 his widow married William Leach, an agricultural labourer. Young William Elias Rolfe became a boot and shoe maker like his father, but decided to leave the Wiltshire countryside to ply his trade in London.

In 1869 Rolfe married Eliza Shears, 20-year-old daughter of boot maker John Shears, at St Philip's Church in Stepney. By the time of the 1871 census the couple had settled at Sutton Street, St George in the East, with their infant son George. Ten years later they were to be found at 24 Cressy Place, Mile End Old Town, with their rapidly growing family. They later moved to 8 Redman Row, in the same district. In 1876 William Rolfe made the decision to join the Metropolitan Police. His service record shows him to have been 5 feet 7 inches tall, barely the minimum height for a police recruit of that time. But what he lacked in height, Rolfe certainly compensated for in astuteness and a dogged commitment to tracking his prey. The *Essex Times* declared that 'Rolfe, although a comparatively young man, has the reputation of being one of the cleverest detectives in the East End of London'.

On the evening of Tuesday 20 January 1885 Rolfe, based at Commercial Street Police Station in Shoreditch, read the telegram from the Essex police giving the first shocking details of the Simmons shooting. He immediately concentrated his energies on finding Dredge, whom he knew by reputation though not by sight. The *Essex Times* related how Rolfe ordered several houses in Whitechapel to be searched. 'Stables and outhouses and all sorts of places were in turn visited by the officer, and the results of his enquiries made it clear to him that the man he was after was in the habit of changing his abode each night.' On Saturday 31 January Rolfe received a tip-off that Dredge could be found at 3 Copperfield Road, a lane leading from Burdett Road in Bow. Accompanied by a fellow detective named Bolton, Rolfe raided the house but no one was at home. Confident that they were on the right track, though, the officers kept the spot under surveillance for the following three days. It could not have been easy for them to remain unnoticed. A contemporary article in the *Graphic* declared that

> There is no denying that most of our detectives are too conspicuous . . . certain men whose looks, dress and general air of having nothing to do mark them out as watchers of other men . . . They appear to be idlers, but do not dress in the style suitable to men who can afford to saunter about with their hands in their pockets.

At last, on Tuesday 3 February, two weeks to the day after the shooting of Simmons, the exertions of the detectives were rewarded. A figure dressed as a dock labourer emerged from 3 Copperfield Road shortly after 9 am. Rolfe only had a photograph to go on, but was certain this was the man he had been hunting. He stepped forward and confronted him.

'I'm a detective officer of the Metropolitan Police. You are David Dredge, wanted, with two others, for the murder of Inspector Simmons of the Essex Constabulary on 20th January.' It was an episode curiously devoid of the drama usually associated with the capture of a dangerous fugitive. Dredge offered no resistance, simply saying 'All right', and was quickly handcuffed. Perhaps, after fourteen days on the run, arrest had been almost a welcome relief; maybe he genuinely believed the police had no case against him.

Dredge meekly asked permission to return home to make himself look 'a little tidy-like'. He led the way to his lodgings, which were quite comfortably furnished and occupied by a woman and four children. Newspapers refer to the lady as Mrs Dredge, but it is unclear whether or not she was Charlotte (nee Eastall) whom he had married seven years before. Rolfe and Bolton kept a strict watch as their captive changed into a brown cloth suit, had a button sewn on his shirt, and bade

Commercial Street Police Station. *Metropolitan Police Historical Collection*

an emotional farewell to his family, exchanging locks of hair with his son. Rolfe then took Dredge by cab to Commercial Street Police Station, where he insisted on making the following statement:

> I never saw Mr Simmons on the 20th. I got out at Rainham station, and was walking along through Rainham when two men overtook me and asked me the way to Romford. I told them that I was going that way, and would show them. When we got near the Cherry Tree public house they asked me to have a drink, but I would not go in.
>
> We walked about two miles towards Romford, and I got over a hedge for a necessary purpose. I heard a cart pass, when a man came through the hedge and said 'David Dredge, what are you doing?' I answered 'You can see what I am doing'. He said 'Come here' and I walked towards him. He then left me

and went away. I came through the hedge and saw a cart about 200 yards down the road. I went to the cart and asked the man who had charge of it where the man was that came over the hedge and spoke to me. I stood at the cart about 20 minutes. I then asked the man 'What is the matter?' He answered 'There were two men gone over the gate and two policemen have gone after them; I think I will wait till they come back, or they may think I have been stealing something.' I then told the man I would mind the cart if he wanted to go. He said 'No, I had better mind it until they come back, or I shall get into a piece of work.' I then said 'I shall not stop any longer, I shall go on my journey.' I never heard a shot fired. The men told me that things were bad for poor people. I don't think I should know them again. All I can say is they looked respectable men.

Rolfe then left for a few hours to attend to a whisky-stealing case at Worship Street Police Court. Dredge had to cool his heels in the cells in the mean time.

The news of the arrest of Dredge was brought to Romford by a man who arrived on the 11.55 am train, and an hour later Inspector Thomas John Cooper, who had been appointed as Simmons's successor, received a confirmatory telegram. Shortly before 2 pm a large crowd outside the station witnessed the arrival of Dredge in the company of Rolfe and Bolton. He was not handcuffed, having given his word that he would give the officers no trouble. Dredge was escorted towards the police station, passing the home of the murdered inspector on the way. Onlookers noted that he appeared quite at ease, speaking cheerfully to his captors about events and places he remembered in Romford from years before, and 'repeatedly laughing at some passing remark'. *The Times* stated that 'The prisoner betrayed no sign of excitement or anxiety on his apprehension, and apparently treated the whole matter with indifference.'

Two hours later Dredge emerged from the police station to be taken back down South Street to the County Court. A crowd of several hundred jostled for a glimpse of him, but were refused entry to the building. When Dredge took his place in the dock he exuded a distinctly sinister aspect – he was described by the *Essex Times* as having 'Black hair which he wears parted down the middle. Overhanging eyebrows and deep-set features.' Dredge's 'well-known black moustache' had been shaved off, but he sported about ten days' growth of beard. He was seen to yawn continuously. Over his brown suit he wore a long black overcoat buttoned up to the neck, a black felt hat and a black scarf.

There was another delay of about an hour before Joseph Fry, chairman of the magistrates, entered the court. Superintendent Dobson rose and announced that, for the time being, he proposed to charge Dredge only with threatening to shoot Marden. Marden then described how he had followed Dredge into the field and had then been threatened with a revolver. Dredge did not take up the offer to put questions to Marden, and was remanded in custody to appear again in two days' time. He was led from the court handcuffed to Sergeant Chase and, accompanied by Superintendent Dobson, Inspector Cooper and several constables, was escorted through a vast crowd to the railway station. By now the mood had turned very hostile indeed. Hisses and yells of a most threatening nature were hurled at Dredge, and the officers must have been tremendously relieved to get their man onto the railway platform and the train to Springfield Gaol at Chelmsford.

That evening a rumour spread around Romford that the other two suspects had been arrested. It soon proved to be unfounded, yet despite this disappointment a positive mood now reigned among the Romford police. Not only was David Dredge safely under lock and key, but Detective Sergeant William Rolfe had offered them hope of a second breakthrough. While waiting for Dredge's appearance before the magistrate, Rolfe had asked Marden to describe once again the man who had pulled the trigger on Simmons. Rolfe had then promptly declared: 'I know his identity. His name is Jim Adams.'

Rolfe then told Superintendent Dobson and the Romford officers why he was so certain of his man. Jim Adams, he explained, was a renowned burglar whose speciality was 'portico thieving'. While the inhabitants of a target house were at dinner downstairs, he would climb the portico over the front door, break in through an upstairs window, drive a wedge under the door to guard against intrusion, and then go to work. Adams and his regular partner in crime Samuel Ellis (nicknamed 'Deaf George') had been sentenced to eight years' penal servitude at the Devon Assizes in March 1871 for housebreaking and wounding with intent to resist arrest. After eight months in a separate cell at Pentonville, Adams was dispatched to Portland Convict Prison. Here he would spend the next five years, and it is likely that this is where he first met Dredge, who had been convicted the previous year.

Criminal records held at the National Archives reveal that Adams was 5 feet $8^{1}/2$ inches tall, with brown hair and deep-set grey-blue eyes. He is stated to have been born at Portsmouth on 1 May 1844. His real origins are obscure, however – in other documents his birthplace is given as County Cork, Ireland, or Brentford in Middlesex. At the time of his arrest he had been living at Plymouth. Adams, a bricklayer by trade, could only read and write 'imperfectly' when first convicted, but educational opportunities were available at Portland in the belief that an educated prisoner was less likely to reoffend. Adams made the most of these, and his progress was rated as 'very good'. Eventually he was transferred from the stone quarrying to a plum job inside the prison bakery. His behaviour occasionally displayed flashes of uncontrollable temper, however. He was three times put in solitary confinement on a 'punishment diet' for fighting with other prisoners. For his part, Adams made an official complaint (which was not upheld) to the Home Office of 'unjust treatment' during his time at Pentonville. Adams was eventually freed in June 1877 on condition that he lived with his mother Ann Adams at 7 Hereford Street in Brighton, and reported to the local police at regular intervals.

Instead of abiding by the rules, however, Adams and Ellis had paid 8 guineas for two of the best revolvers at Reilly's gun shop in London's High Holborn and returned to their old trade with redoubled vigour. Early in 1878 they were the prime suspects for a raid on the home of Mr Spencer Charrington, the Ilford brewer, in which property worth £800 was taken. Close to midnight on 9 May that year they were spotted by two police officers named Child and Seats in a lane at Quedgeley, Gloucestershire, suspiciously close to a large country house. The policemen demanded to search the pair, whose response was to whip out revolvers and open fire. A bullet whizzed past the head of PC Child, and his companion was hit in the knee. The gunmen then escaped.

Rolfe then described to the Romford officers how a month later, in June 1878, he and Detective Inspector Richard Wildey had managed to arrest Samuel Ellis in the Mile End Road, Whitechapel. Ellis was sent back to Gloucestershire on a charge of wounding Thomas Child with intent to murder, found guilty and sentenced to penal servitude for life. Yet for Rolfe the job remained unfinished. During the seven years that had followed, his overriding ambition, amounting to obsession, had been the capture of Jim Adams. He later admitted: 'I knew him too well, unfortunately for me. He worried me enough for years.'

Adams, meanwhile, reportedly declared that he would rather be 'topped' (executed) than return to 'pushing a barrow', the slang term for convict labour which he and Dredge had undergone at Portland. His name continued to be linked to spectacular crimes. A jeweller's shop in Doncaster was emptied on the day of the St Leger horse race; a police constable in Northampton was lucky to escape with his life when a bullet went clean through his helmet; an old lady was found with her throat cut at the foot of the stairs in her home at Old Ford, robbed of about £70. Adams also supposedly admitted having shot a man by the side of a canal and pushed the body into the water, then being highly amused when a coroner's jury returned a verdict of 'found drowned'. Adams may not, of course, have been responsible for all the misdeeds attributed to him, but they reinforced his reputation as one of the most dangerous men in the country. He apparently knew that William Rolfe was on a personal mission to arrest him, and took care never to be without a six-chambered revolver in his pocket and a dagger in his waistcoat.

Detective Sergeant Rolfe then explained to Dobson that on the morning following the shooting of Thomas Simmons he had read the description of the other gunman in the newspapers. He had no doubt about his identity. 'I told my superintendent that I believed Adams was the man who had committed the murder', he recalled. 'I did not mince matters.'

7

'What Sort of Revolver was it?'

Two days later David Dredge was brought back from Chelmsford to face the Romford magistrates once more. Dredge was, of course, no stranger to courtrooms, and was no doubt fully conversant with legal procedures. In the short time he had been on remand he had wisely obtained a solicitor, Mr W T Bateson, who had in turn engaged a defence barrister, Mr Philip Stern. The services of such an advocate would normally have been beyond the financial reach of a man such as Dredge, described in the indictment as 'a dealer, of Burdett Road'. Stern, however, was very much an outsider in London legal circles, and would eventually forge himself a reputation for defending anti-establishment figures. It is possible that having read about the case in the newspapers, he had volunteered his services at a greatly reduced fee or even for free. Born into a Jewish family in Kingston, Jamaica, Stern had been educated at University College London before being called to the Bar in June 1869. He had chambers at 5 Essex Court in the Temple, and was celebrating his thirty-eighth birthday that very day, 5 February 1885.

It was announced that Dredge was charged with threatening to shoot PC Marden. Having appeared on numerous occasions before some formidable judges, Philip Stern was not intimidated in the slightest by their Worships Messrs. Fry and Price. Clad in his legal garb of wig and gown, he rose and went straight on the offensive. 'I ought, perhaps, to mention that I appear for the prisoner. I was under the impression that he was charged with murder. I am not at all surprised that the prosecution, in their wisdom, have determined to drop the more serious charge.' Henry Haynes, as well as being coroner for the Liberty, was also clerk to the magistrates, responsible for advising them on matters of law and procedure. He stole some of Mr Stern's thunder with 'I don't think you can entirely say that yet'. Mr Fry added that 'The charge is only dropped for the present.' Alfred Marden was then called to repeat his evidence, but was not cross-examined. The proceedings at an end for the time being, David Dredge was whisked back to Springfield Gaol.

Later that evening, a further meeting of the Simmons Fund Committee was held at the Golden Lion. The Reverend Hitchcock enthused, 'Gentlemen, I cannot help expressing my great satisfaction that one, at least, of the three men engaged in this wretched murder of our excellent Inspector has been captured since our last meeting.' His statement was greeted with hearty 'Hear, Hears'. The vicar gave the news that the fund was growing steadily day by day, now amounting to almost £150.

Meanwhile, it was announced that the Essex Constabulary had agreed to pay the medical bills incurred for the care of Thomas Simmons during his final days, amounting to over £30. A further piece of news, much less welcome to the people of Romford, was that the Treasury refused to add a single shilling to the reward for information leading to the conviction of the killers. The *Chelmsford Chronicle* noted that the decision 'has been the subject of much surprise and dissatisfaction, as it is felt that this is peculiarly a case in which their powerful aid should be given to bring the murderers to justice'.

On Thursday 12 February David Dredge was brought before the Romford magistrates for the third time. Philip Stern now unleashed a scathing criticism of the conduct so far of the case against his client. He pointed out that there were no independent witnesses to what had occurred when Marden had confronted Dredge in the field. Why on earth, he demanded, were the magistrates dragging out the proceedings by repeatedly remanding Dredge in custody? Stern claimed that all this did was to give Marden ample time to amend his account should he be disposed to do so. He warned that 'The police are directly connected with this case, and the temptation of those persons who were present to obtain the missing link in the evidence is too great, and ought not to be placed in the way of the Constable or anyone else.' Stern also objected to newspapers flagrantly

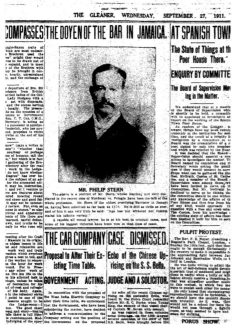

Philip Stern, defence counsel for David Dredge, as pictured in *The Gleaner*.

branding Dredge a murderer while he, of course, remained innocent until proven otherwise.

Stern's protests cut no ice with the bench. Mr Fry stated that, 'Considering the gravity of the case, every possible power will be given to the prosecution. As a further remand is thought necessary, I shall grant it.' Philip Stern was unperturbed. He had fully anticipated their Worships' ruling; realistically he could have expected no other. He would, however, be given the opportunity to question Marden. Throughout his long career, one of the fiercest adversaries Marden would face, and one he would long remember, was to be Mr Philip Stern.

Marden's previous statement regarding the events of 20 January was read over. Stern immediately put a string of questions regarding the dates on which he had previously been examined. The rapidity of the questioning seemed to disconcert the officer, and Mr Haynes felt compelled to intervene. 'I don't think the witness quite understands your question.'

'That is part of my case,' responded Stern, 'I want to know what he really does know, and whether he understands much about it at all!' The gloves were now off, and the pages of the *Essex Times* reveal a remarkable altercation which, had it been staged in less dire circumstances, verged closely on becoming a music-hall comedy.

Dobson weighed in with 'Surely Sir, this witness ought to be treated as a proper and truthful witness. He is a witness of truth and his evidence is still within the knowledge of the Court. I can pledge myself to this, that he gives truthful evidence.'

Stern was indignant. 'I am surprised at these proceedings. Because he is responsible for the prosecution, the Superintendent gets up and pledges himself for the truth of the witness and interferes with my cross-examination. The witness is to be left in my hands. I wish, however, only to do justice to the prisoner and witness, but I will not be interfered with by a constable in this way.'

Joseph Fry protested that 'Marden is a highly respectable officer, and his evidence ought not to be discredited.' Stern, however, gave no ground. 'I know nothing about the man. I must ask questions.' Haynes retorted: 'I shall not take the answers unless the questions are such as the witness understands.'

'But they will be taken by others.' Turning sharply back to Marden, Stern demanded 'What sort of revolver was it the prisoner pointed at you?'

'The same as any other. I know a revolver when I see one.'

'I didn't ask you that sir!' snapped Stern, 'Can you give me any description of it?'

Marden hesitated, and Mr Fry advised him not to try to describe the weapon unless he could do so accurately. 'No sir, I can't' conceded Marden eventually.

Stern now turned to the matter of the pony and trap, making the point that

Dredge had not run away from the scene, as a guilty man might have done, but had remained talking with Kemp for some considerable time. 'It is very important that you, a *highly respectable* officer, should take care what you say and know. Will you undertake to swear that the prisoner, Dredge, did not hold the horse?'

'I do not know. He did not, at any rate, in my presence', Marden answered.

'That won't do for me. I must have it my style!' raged Stern, 'You will not undertake to swear that the prisoner did not hold the horse?'

'I will not swear it', Marden persisted.

After some discussion about whether Marden had ever seen Dredge before the day of the shooting, Stern changed tack. 'What time of day was it when you met the men? Was it moonlight?'

'No, sir, it was daylight.'

'You will swear to that?'

'I will.'

After enquiring innocently whether Marden lived in Romford, Stern suddenly demanded 'Did you run away from these men?'

'No, Sir, I ran to the assistance of my late Inspector.'

'But don't you know it has been said that you ran away?' Stern asked, provocatively.

'No, I am not the man to run away!' replied the irate constable.

'Have you between 20th January and 5th February discussed this case with anyone?'

'No, sir.'

'How do you fix the time at ten minutes to five?'

'I know by the time I passed the Cherry Tree public house. I often passed the public house, and I guessed the time from that.'

'You are sure you are not guessing anything else?'

'Yes I am.'

'Of course, you did not go in?'

'Yes, I did', admitted the officer.

'And did you have anything to drink?' Stern asked mischievously.

Marden sprang to the defensive. 'That is my business!' he snarled. In the dock, David Dredge must have been grinning inwardly at the constable's discomfiture. His counsel's baiting of the policeman was proceeding very successfully.

'What is that? You on oath, and answer in that way? This is the most extraordinary unchecked demeanour I have ever heard.'

Marden looked over at Haynes. 'You must answer yes or no', he was told. Stern pressed the point: 'Surely such an answer as that is not going to be allowed to pass without any reproof?' The tone of the proceedings now became even more heated. 'I have already told the witness his duty is to answer you,' said Mr Haynes, 'but I must say you have brought this on yourself. One or two of your observations were totally improper, and if counsel for the other side had been present, you would have been checked long before this.' He continued: 'If that is not sufficient for you, Sir, I shall refuse to take down any evidence whenever such question is put. You have no right to insinuate anything.'

Stern denied making insinuations, and Haynes retorted that he might decide not to take down the answers to his questions. Stern snapped: 'I have tried to do everything to carry on the case consistently and according to the law, but when a witness tells a counsel it is "his business", I am bound to find out.'

Haynes replied: 'He has been reprimanded; but the question is most unjustifiable.' Stern turned back to Marden, and repeated 'Did you have anything to drink?' The officer reluctantly answered: 'I did, I had a glass of ale.' 'Are you certain it was not two?' 'I will swear it was not!'

Marden was eventually allowed to stand down. The verbal hostilities, however, went on between Stern and Haynes. 'There is one thing I shall ask, and that is to have the depositions read over', said Stern haughtily. 'I noticed this was not done on the last occasion.'

'I know what I am about', said the piqued Mr Haynes.

Stern saw an opportunity to score further points. 'I can allow for this feeling, seeing as the Inspector was so highly respected.' What had, hitherto, merely seemed professional animosity between two opposing factions now manifested itself as an unconcealed, bitter mutual loathing. 'There is no feeling, sir, on the part of the Court, nor on mine, and you have no right to insinuate such a thing', burst out Haynes. 'Your remarks and behaviour are most disgraceful!'

Stern eyed him contemptuously. 'You speak as if you were someone of authority in this place. I assure you I take no notice of what you say'. 'All I ask is that you will behave properly!' said Haynes. 'I will talk to you downstairs, sir, and not here.' 'What! I am surprised at your conduct. You shall hear further about this.' Eventually Mr Fry had to interrupt. 'I think enough words have been said on this matter'.

Bail was refused. Dredge, remanded for a further week, was ushered out of the building. He would sleep a little easier in his prison bed that night with the reassuring knowledge that the accomplished Mr Philip Stern was in his corner. Stern himself would vent his feelings about Mr Haynes (taking care not to actually name him) in a series of scathing articles for *Pump Court*, a legal magazine of which he was editor.

During the hearing press reporters noted that David Dredge's wife, 'who wept bitterly throughout the proceedings, occupied a seat on one of the front benches'. Two days later, on Saturday 14 February, she opened the door of her home in Copperfield Road, Bow, to find Detective Sergeant Rolfe and Superintendent Dobson asking to speak to her. Rolfe had brought two portraits of Adams — one a woodcut, the other a photograph obtained from Scotland Yard five days previously. He told Mrs Dredge of his belief that the murderer of Simmons was Jim Adams, whose bearded face stared out from the photograph he handed to her. 'Do you know him?' Rolfe held his breath. Would his theory be proved right?

Mrs Dredge looked up. 'Yes', she replied. 'But not as Adams. I know him as Manson, he is living in that name.' She told them he had visited her house several times. She was aware that he carried a revolver and was a dangerous man.

'Do you know where he lives?' asked Rolfe.

'Near Plaistow Railway Station, I believe. He told me he moved there about Christmas.'

Knowing that pawn tickets were traded like cash, Rolfe asked Mrs Dredge whether Adams/Manson had ever offered her a ticket with his address on. Yes, she replied, one for a shilling, and the address on it was, she believed, Medburn Street.

On leaving, the delighted Rolfe and Dobson headed straight to Bow Street Police Station and pulled a London street atlas from the shelves. Medburn Street, they found, was close to Euston Station. Rolfe's heart must have leapt at this news. As we have seen, the glasses case inside the gunman's discarded coat bore the label of optician John Salmon of 24 Seymour Street, Euston Square. Rolfe had already spoken to Mr Salmon, whose sales book revealed that the case had been sold on 30 December the previous year. Mrs Elizabeth Salmon remembered the customer, a man accompanied by a boy aged about 7. She recalled that, on leaving, the man had turned and disputed the change: 'My little boy tells me that I gave you a sovereign.' Mrs Salmon told him firmly that it was not the case. The man then put his hand in his pocket and pulled out the coin, which was worth £1. 'Oh, it's all right', he told her. 'I know I had a sovereign.'

Rolfe and Dobson travelled to Medburn Street and quizzed its inhabitants. They were not poor; the Booth Poverty Map of 1898–9 classifies the street as 'Fairly comfortable. Good ordinary earnings.' Neighbours confirmed that the Mansons had indeed lived at number 24, but had since moved a short distance to 36 Clarendon Street. On going to that address, the officers once again found no sign of their quarry. They were told that the family had departed for Plaistow, East London (confirming what Mrs Dredge had said), but, alas, no specific forwarding address had been given.

Rolfe and Dobson considered their next move. Their suspect's fondness for pawnshops had already provided one breakthrough, in the form of the Medburn Street address. Perhaps it would lead them even closer to him in due course. Pawnbrokers' shops were often used as a source of ready money by burglars in the fallow periods between 'jobs'. The pair accordingly did the rounds of such shops, armed with the woodcut and photograph of Adams. Although the fugitive had last been reported heading towards Plaistow, Rolfe had a hunch that he would be drawn back to his familiar haunts in the Camden and Euston area. Consequently on Monday 16 February, two days after their meeting with Mrs Dredge, Rolfe and Dobson called at Mr Theodore Lawley's shop at 128 Seymour Street, Euston Square.

The senior assistant at Lawley's and described as 'practically the manager', was 23-year-old Edward Alfred Baxter, born and raised in Clapham in South London. Baxter declared that yes, he recognized the face in the photograph, though since it was taken the man had shaved off his beard. 'He is a commercial traveller, and I believe he is a respectable man.' Baxter agreed that the man's name was James Manson and the address he had given was 24 Medburn Street.

'Has he ever pledged a revolver?' asked Dobson. Baxter stated that he had, and after checking the transaction book was able to confirm that Adams/Manson had pawned a revolver for a few weeks towards the end of the previous year.

Dobson declared to Baxter and his shocked staff that their customer was sought on suspicion of murdering Thomas Simmons. Rolfe then instructed them on what to do if Adams returned. The staff were to send word to nearby Platt Street Police Station and try to keep the suspect waiting until the arrival of the police. Rolfe explained that Adams was an educated man, 'a bit of a politician and fond of reading a paper'. One of the shop assistants agreed, saying that Adams had once stood for twenty minutes immersed in a newspaper, and it was decided that copies should be prominently placed at the counter.

Rolfe and Dobson then went straight to Platt Street Station to inform the officers what was happening. 'I told them to be careful with him', recalled Rolfe, 'as he was a ruffian'. The detective probably also feared that, with more people now aware of the net closing in around the target, details might be leaked to the newspapers, putting Adams on his guard and perhaps causing him to flee London altogether. At the time, Metropolitan Police officers were being accused of selling information about the hunt for the men behind the recent London bomb attacks, thus jeopardizing the investigation. The *Graphic* of 24 January 1885 thundered:

Some of our London policemen would be the better for being wholly dumb if, as is alleged, they have been communicating to newspaper reporters their

Horse-drawn cabs waiting at the foot of the slope leading up to Romford Station.
London Borough of Havering Local Studies

discoveries of dynamite outrage-plotters . . . Policemen have thus come to learn that news is a marketable commodity . . . the policeman, who, having discovered dynamite or overheard conspirators chatting, is clearly unfit for his work. He is a survival of the old watchmen, whose duty was associated with that of the town crier.

Back at Romford, on Thursday 19 February, David Dredge appeared before the magistrates for the fourth time. The *Essex Weekly News* reported that 'The Court and its environs were densely crowded, and the greatest interest was excited to catch a view of the accused.' Dredge must have been somewhat disquieted when barrister Michael Sydney Batchelor, representing the Director of Public Prosecutions, announced that 'The prisoner is now charged for the crime of wilful murder and that is the charge upon which I propose to proceed today.' On hearing these words, the colour drained visibly from Dredge's face, leaving him deathly pale. If convicted of this charge, which, given the climate of public feeling against him in the county, seemed increasingly probable, only the gallows could await him. At the front of the court Philip Stern sat coolly concentrating on his legal books and documents. Outwardly unmoved, he knew he was going to have his work cut out.

Mr Batchelor went on to outline the case for the prosecution, indicating that he would proceed on the premise that Dredge had been in company with the two others for a common purpose. If all had been armed with revolvers, then under such circumstances Dredge was equally guilty of wilful murder as the man who had fired the fatal shot. In the dock, Dredge must have felt a cold shudder run down his spine as Batchelor went on to cite a case in Manchester some years earlier. Three Fenian activists had tried to break into a prison van to free two of their comrades. One had fired at the lock, but the bullet had penetrated the door and killed a police sergeant, Charles Brett. Though only one had pulled the trigger, all three had been hanged.[12]

Mr Batchelor went on to claim that 'the object of Dredge when he went to Kemp . . . and offered to take charge of the Inspector's horse and cart was, no doubt, to get into the cart, drive away, and so escape'. A plan of the location of the shooting, drawn by Brentwood auctioneer and surveyor Abraham Thorne, was passed round. Marden, Matthews and Kemp were called to restate their testimony, but Philip Stern declined to cross-examine them that day. He knew that his most important task now was to oppose the argument that Dredge was as guilty in law as the man who had fired the bullet. Dredge was remanded for a further week.

Seven days later, on 26 February, David Dredge was again brought by train to Romford to take his familiar place in the dock. Evidence from the remaining witnesses having been heard, Philip Stern launched into a riposte to Mr Batchelor's argument, declaring that: 'The story of *Oliver Twist* went to show how an innocent person could be connected with the guilty, unknown to himself.' The onus was on the prosecution, he maintained, to prove that it had been a shared enterprise. Dredge could not, argued Stern, be held responsible for the reckless action of the others when he was such a considerable distance from them at the time. 'Nobody suggests that he was present when the poor unfortunate inspector lost his life.'

Joseph Fry, however, was not to be moved. 'We do not think we can take the responsibility of withholding the case from a jury. The prisoner is committed for trial at the next assizes at Chelmsford.' As a buzz of voices echoed around the packed courtroom, the stunned and subdued David Dredge was removed to Romford Station to await the two o'clock train to Chelmsford. Philip Stern set off in the opposite direction, back to his chambers in the Temple to begin his preparations for the defence of the man whose life now depended entirely on his ability as a barrister.

8

'Man Detained: Come At Once'

It was now the beginning of March 1885, two weeks after Rolfe and Dobson had visited the pawnbroker's shop, and still James Adams eluded them. At last, a long-awaited breakthrough came when the detectives managed to trace the removal man who had taken the family's goods from Clarendon Street. Apparently they had moved on 3 January, and their new address was 15 Caistor Park Road, Plaistow. Rolfe and Dobson headed straight there, only to find the bird had flown again.

They spoke to Charles Henry Woodcraft, who lived two doors away at 19 Caistor Park Road. He remembered the family well, having decorated the house for them. They had remained just under three weeks, leaving between 9.30 and 10 am on 23 January, three days after the shooting of Simmons. The family had been gone for two days when Woodcraft became worried about water pouring out of the back of the house. He climbed in through a window, found a tap still running and turned it off. Woodcraft told the detectives that on 5 January he had called and found Adams/Manson about to go out, dressed in a long overcoat, a white wrapper and black felt hat. He had spotted him another day at Plaistow Railway Station, again wearing the coat. On seeing the coat dropped by the gunman, Woodcraft declared he was certain they were one and the same.

Rolfe and Dobson now joined forces with 36-year-old K Division Detective Sergeant George Mellish, who provided an invaluable knowledge of the area. Their enquiries soon revealed that the family's destination on 23 January had been 10 London Terrace, just a short distance away. Once more their stay had been short, for on 25 February, Ash Wednesday, Adams had hired a removal van, packed their goods and left at ten o'clock at night. House-to-house enquiries were made, and on 9 March Rolfe and Mellish spoke to a greengrocer who gave them the welcome news that his van had been hired to move the family's goods. Their destination had been Ferdinand Place, off Grange Road in Chalk Farm, north-west London, not far from their former home at Medburn Street.

The elation felt by Rolfe and Mellish was tempered by news of a tragedy that had occurred in the early hours of the morning that very day, Monday, 9 March.

Detective Sergeant George Mellish. *Metropolitan Police Historical Collection*

Their colleague, 28-year-old H Division Detective Richard James Barber, had been pursuing two suspected burglars at a railway goods yard at Royal Mint Street, Whitechapel. He followed the men across the roofs of the goods sheds and nearby houses. Barber closed in on one of the suspects and was about to grab him when he fell through a glass roof 30 feet to the stone floor below. He was taken to the London Hospital but died a few hours later. Rolfe and Mellish may well have gone to Leman Street Police Station to pay their respects at Barber's open coffin, which had been placed in the library. The *Illustrated Police News* reported that 'The body was fearfully mutilated, the unfortunate officer having fallen on his head.' Barber's funeral the following Saturday at the City of London Cemetery was attended by 'large contingents from the various divisions', and Leman Street and the Commercial Road were crowded with spectators.

On the morning of Tuesday 10 March Rolfe prepared to tighten the snare around Adams by raiding the Ferdinand Place address. Before he could strike, however, events took an unexpected turn. A young assistant named Hunniman was on duty at Theodore Lawley's pawnbroker's shop when just after 8 am a man wearing a black cut-away coat and brown striped trousers asked to pawn a revolver for 10 shillings. The lad nipped into the back office and told Edward Baxter he thought Adams was in the shop. Baxter whispered that he would come through and nudge Hunniman's foot if it was the right man. He duly did so, and Hunniman went into the street via the shop next door and ran to Platt Street Police Station.

Baxter placed the revolver on the back counter and held Adams in conversation, asking him how his wife and family were. Adams then mentioned a watch he had pledged earlier, and Baxter immediately offered to go down to the jewellery safe for it. Despite Adams's protestations that he was in a hurry and it didn't matter, Baxter played for time by fetching the watch. Adams repeated that he had no time to spare, so Baxter began to write out the pawn ticket for the revolver. About ten minutes had passed since Adams had entered the shop. Baxter was just handing over the ticket when two uniformed police constables, Edwin Day and William Allaway, strode in.

'I believe this man has offered a revolver to pledge?' asked Day. Baxter answered that yes, he had.

'Hand it to me', demanded the officer.

'I've pawned this here before, haven't I Alfred?' pleaded Adams.

Day put the revolver in his pocket and announced he was arresting Adams to the station 'on suspicion of shooting Inspector Simmons, at Romford'.

'You must be mad!' he replied, but agreed to go with them.

The constables each grabbed their captive by the collar on either side and led him sideways out of the door. The moment they were outside, however, Adams tripped up PC Day with his left foot. As the officer fell he tried and failed to drag Adams down with him. Adams then tried unsuccessfully to trip Allaway with his right foot, but managed to pull free from his grasp and dash across the road. The constables gave chase, and on reaching the corner of Bedford Street, some twenty yards from the shop, Allaway had almost caught up with the fugitive. Suddenly Adams collided with a passer-by, who saw what was happening and held on to him. Adams continued to put up a furious struggle, but the policemen eventually got him in handcuffs and dragged him to Platt Street Police Station.

While a telegram was being sent to the CID, Adams was left in the charge room rather than locked in a cell. His wily mind scanned it for opportunities of escape. He had clearly not been thoroughly searched, for the moment he sensed he was unobserved he took out a small bag concealed within his coat. It contained about a dozen bullets, and Adams immediately threw a handful into the room's roaring fire. After a few seconds they exploded, and in the resulting pandemonium Adams made a bid for the door. It took several officers to overpower the desperate man, but he was eventually secured to await the arrival of the detectives. He was searched and four keys were found on him, one a skeleton key.

Meanwhile, at Commercial Street Police Station, William Rolfe could hardly believe his eyes when a telegram arrived from Platt Street, reading 'Man detained; come at once; supposed to be Adams.' Shortly after one o'clock Rolfe arrived and took his first look at the glowering prisoner. He recalled that he 'identified him at once as the man I wanted. I told him "You will be charged with the murder of

Inspector Simmons", to which he made no answer to the charge, but called me a pig.' Rolfe and PC Day took Adams by cab to Commercial Street Police Station. He continued to deny any involvement in the killing. 'I don't know anything about it in any shape or form. It is the dirty dogs that know me that have got me into this.' Rolfe and Day waited for the arrival of Mellish, then took their prisoner, arms handcuffed behind his back, on an underground train to Liverpool Street Station. The group then caught the 2.47 pm Great Eastern service to Romford.

Rolfe had sent a telegram in advance, and in Romford the news spread like wildfire. The *Essex Times* commented that 'Though seven weeks have elapsed since the fatal shot was fired by the assassin, the interest of the public has remained undiminished.' The train pulled in at 3.24 pm, and spectators craned their necks for a glimpse of Adams. According to the *Essex Times* he had 'a most repulsive countenance'. Another newspaper noted his 'very determined appearance' and that 'it is evident that he has been in want'. Inspector Cooper, Sergeant Chase and two Romford constables met the captive and his escort. As the party made their way along South Street to the police station they would have passed Cavendish Villa. Were Mary Simmons and her children inside, listening to the jeers and hisses of the assembled throng? Adams replied to the hostile demonstration with defiant sneers and grimaces.

James Adams photographed in Pentonville Prison. The photograph on the left was taken at the beginning of his sentence in 1871, and the other shortly before he was released in 1877. *The National Archives*

On reaching the police station with the long-awaited suspect, Superintendent Dobson's mood of celebration must have soon turned rather sour. A knotty problem now presented itself – that of identification. Adams had given his name as James Lee and his age 45. He refused to supply an address or occupation. In that year of 1885, the technique of fingerprinting had not yet been developed, and DNA testing lay a whole century in the future. Proper identification of suspects was a constant difficulty for the police.

Dobson needed to hold an identity parade before asking a magistrate to formally charge Adams. Asserting his right to justice and impartiality, however, the prisoner adamantly refused to line up alongside any men not complete strangers to the area. He asserted that 'If Romford men were placed beside him they would be known to Marden and the other witnesses and his chances would be nil.' He also pointed out, quite reasonably, that 'after having been dragged through the streets of the town, and seen by about half the population, Marden or anyone else would have no difficulty in identifying him'.

Dobson was put in the embarrassing position of having to go to Romford Railway Station and delay trains while he asked passengers passing through to volunteer for the identity parade. He 'begged in the most imploring tones' for gentlemen 'to assist him on a matter of urgent and pressing importance'. Adams firmly objected to the use of any men not of the same height and general appearance as himself. 'Because the strangers did not, as the prisoner did, happen to wear a moustache and no beard, or that they were stout whilst he was thin, he still pressed his objections'.

After three hours an acceptable line-up had still not been found. Joseph Fry had long since returned to his home at Hornchurch, leaving his fellow-magistrate Ralph Price kicking his heels at the County Court waiting in vain to open a formal hearing. After talking the matter over with Dobson, Price agreed to go to the police station and verbally remand Adams for two days on a charge of murder. The formalities over, Adams was brought out and put in a cab with Rolfe, Mellish and Cooper. Superintendent Dobson climbed on top with the driver, and the vehicle edged through South Street towards the railway station. Crowds pressed around on all sides, jeering and hissing, and Adams responded by shouting 'If I'd my liberty you would not do that!' He was eventually put on board the 7.35 pm train to Chelmsford, en route for Springfield Gaol.

In the following issue of the *Essex Times* a headline proclaimed: 'CAPTURE OF THE MURDERER. THE "TALL MAN" IN CUSTODY.' The *Essex Weekly News*, on the other hand, noted that Adams was nowhere near the height of the gunman, described as a six-footer. It assumed that Adams was the second fugitive, the man described on the placards as 'About 33 years of age, 5ft 7in high, clean shaved, hair inclined to be ginger, in round felt hat, and short dark jacket.' The newspaper told its readers that 'this description is in many respects fully answered by the present appearance of the accused, except that he has now a full flowing moustache, slightly tinged with red, whilst his hair is brown, the other portions of his face being closely shaved'.

Exactly why James Adams chose the pseudonym of Lee may never be known, but Fred Feather, former curator of the Essex Police Museum, offers an intriguing theory in his essay *The Amateur Hangman*:

> On 23 February 1885 a bizarre event occurred at Exeter Gaol. A man named John Lee should have been executed but the gallows failed to work on three occasions and he was reprieved. He was then known as 'Lee, the man they could not hang'. . . Is it possible that he [Adams] thought the defiant use of the name might keep him from Executioner Berry's clutches?

The *Globe and Traveller* gave the startling information that 'Not only was he recognized by Sergeant Rolfe but he is said to be "wanted" at Southampton, Gloucester and Bristol'. The *Chelmsford Chronicle* commented that 'But for the fact that he was starved out and so compelled to part with his terrible weapon, the story of his apprehension would probably have been bound up with another tragedy.' Readers of the *Essex Times* were told:

> It is asserted that friends of the prisoner had subscribed £40 to enable him to get away, but that Adams refused to go; and incredible as it may appear, it is related, on what seems to be a trustworthy source, that a day or two before the arrest of Dredge, Adams and a friend of his proposed to get him on a journey by train when they intended to shoot him in a tunnel and throw his body out of the train.

Now that the news blackout on his pursuit of Adams was no longer necessary, newspapers were full of praise for William Rolfe. The *Chelmsford Chronicle* declared that he had 'shown great perseverance and ingenuity in getting upon the track . . . and following him up'. The *Essex Weekly News* noted that Rolfe 'has been indefatigable in his endeavours during the last five weeks to trace the residence of the accused'.

On Wednesday 11 March, the day after the arrest of Adams, Rolfe, Mellish and Dobson made their way to his lodgings at 27 Ferdinand Place in Chalk Farm. They found his wife Charlotte and four children living in two rooms in the direst poverty, with hardly any furniture. The wife cut a pitiable figure, sewing a calico cover to put on her bedspread before taking it to the pawnshop. It seems that she had lived in complete ignorance of her husband's criminal career. She had known him only a few weeks when they married by licence on 29 August 1877 at St Pancras Church. The bridegroom had represented himself as James Manson, aged 28, a baker of 61 Judd Street, son of the late John Manson, a blacking maker. His bride, 27-year-old Charlotte Kitchen, was the daughter of the late Charles Kitchen, a coach builder. Although Charlotte's occupation was not given on the marriage certificate, she was a domestic servant who claimed to have worked for several years in the household of Lady Rolle at Bicton in Devon.

At the time of their marriage, James had told Charlotte that he was giving up his job as a baker. He would now be working as a commercial traveller for a firm of blacking manufacturers that had employed his father for many years. James would frequently be away for up to two months at a time, supposedly on business. During these absences he never failed to send money home each week. The 1881 census shows them at 24 Medburn Street. Head of the family, James Manson, gives his age as 32 and his birthplace as Brentford, Middlesex. His occupation is listed as 'Traveller glass'. His wife is 31 and born in Northamptonshire, and their children are George, 3, and one-year-old Catherine. Their remaining children were to be Charlotte, born in 1882, and James, only nine days old when his father was captured.

When Rolfe, Mellish and Dobson entered the Ferdinand Place house, Charlotte's mother and sister also happened to be there, perhaps helping to care for the newborn baby. The sister later complained on Charlotte's behalf that 'I know policemen must do their duty, but they might have a little sympathy for a poor woman in her trouble, but they showed none'. The *Chelmsford Chronicle* and other newspapers alleged that Adams's mother-in-law had exclaimed: 'I thank God my prayers are answered at last. For five years I have been praying to see my daughter in widow's weeds. Five years I have prayed for it; and at last I am answered.' Presumably this colourful account emanated from an interview with one of the officers. She was quoted as asking them to treat her daughter with respect: 'Remember that though she is poor, she is a lady.' Newspapers also reported that Dobson gave Mrs Adams money from his own pocket so that she could buy food.

The detectives undertook a systematic search of the house. In a drawer Mellish found a long palette knife, two wedges, two gimlets, a small piece of candle and a pair of padded socks. He immediately recognized them as essential tools of a burglar's trade. The long, thin-bladed knife would have been used to release the catches of sash windows. The gimlets secured the wedges beneath doors to prevent entry from outside. The candle would afford a tiny, almost imperceptible light while the padded socks would enable silent movement around a house in the small hours of the night.

9

'Simply the Victim of Police Hatred and Malice'

The following morning, Thursday 12 March, a proper identity parade was held in the yard at Chelmsford prison. Most of the twenty or so participants were workers at the nearby Arc Electric factory. Alfred Marden inspected the men first. He went straight up to Adams and said 'This is the man'. The line-up was then reshuffled before PC Emery appeared, but he too picked out Adams almost immediately. Frederick Wilderspin, who had seen the suspects at Rainham Railway Station, was called next. He passed up and down the row twice before choosing Adams, who was also identified by his ex-neighbour, Charles Woodcraft. Matthews, Kemp and Sawkins, the sewage farm labourers who had had a close view of Simmons's assailants, did not pick out anyone from the line-up. Mrs Salmon, the optician's wife, went past Adams and tapped the shoulder of a different man.

The identity parade over, Adams was taken to Chelmsford station for the journey to Romford. In the waiting room he was seen talking 'in a semi-sympathetic manner' with his arch-enemy Rolfe, asking about the prison visiting times, and begging the detective to urge his wife to come to Springfield and see him. In Romford a large crowd had gathered, expecting Adams on the 8.39 am train, on which Dredge had usually arrived. As the *Essex Weekly News* put it, 'The hundreds of persons . . . who, in the hope of making prisoner's acquaintance had left a warm breakfast table to face a keen East Wind, were doomed to disappointment.' The crowd had diminished by the time Adams's train eventually steamed in at 11.29, but many remained to jeer and hoot as he was escorted along South Street to the County Court.

Adams was furious with Superintendent Dobson for not putting him in a cab away from the public gaze. On arrival at the court he refused to sit down, shouting: 'Here's a man who has to be identified, and he is obliged to walk through the streets in front of everyone again . . . I want it to be known how they treated me. The rabble in the streets hooted at me like wild beasts . . . They are savage beasts. They are not human…It's persecution. It's nothing else . . . I call this damned unfair!' His face was white with rage.

The normally dignified Joseph Fry had to retort 'Hold your tongue!' PC Edwin Day, who had arrested Adams, was the only witness to be called, and gave his evidence amidst a barrage of interruptions and mocking comments from Adams in the dock. The magistrates announced that Adams was remanded in custody for a further week. Inevitably, he was quick to protest.

'I know why the remand is asked for. They want to manipulate the evidence . . . Why don't you take a man out and shoot him at once? That's what you are doing!'

'You will have justice', assured Mr Fry.

'I shall have plenty of law, but no justice. Am I to sit here and be trodden upon like a worm?' Pointing at Dobson, he yelled 'You are a gross brute, you are! That's your treatment throughout. That's the way you manipulate evidence to hang an innocent man!'

As his train left Romford Station at 1.50 pm on the way back to Chelmsford, Adams stood at the window, raising his hat and bowing in mock acknowledgement of the hissing crowd on the platform.

Five days later, on Tuesday 17 March, a concert was held at Dunmow Town Hall in aid of the Simmons Fund. Performers included six members of the Dunmow Brass Band and a Mr Mortimer delighting the audience with his piccolo solos. We

The entrance gate of Chelmsford Gaol. *Essex Record Office*

are also told that 'Mr E. J. Wilton sang "the Powder Monkey" in his best style'. The event raised £12.

At 11 am on Thursday 19 March James Adams was again brought before the Romford magistrates. The court was crowded, and it was reported that 'some ladies occupied seats near the bench'. Adams sat waiting with head bowed while other, less important, business was transacted. The *Essex Weekly News* noted that, though still defiant, 'Prisoner appeared thin and care-worn, and had lost that vulgar daring that characterised his former appearances'. Adams announced that he had written to the Home Office asking for legal assistance, and wanted a further remand until he should have a defence barrister to cross-examine witnesses on his behalf. As we have seen, Adams had been utterly destitute at the time of his arrest, and had only attempted to pawn the revolver as a last resort. Being unable to afford a defence lawyer had put him at a considerable disadvantage. A barrister of the calibre of Philip Stern would probably have questioned some of the procedures employed by the police and may, perhaps, have been able to introduce a vestige of reasonable doubt into the proceedings.

'Indeed, we should prefer that you were represented,' said Mr Fry. 'Our only object is to do justice.' He refused to grant an immediate remand, however, declaring that witnesses could give evidence that day and be cross-examined by the defence on a future occasion.

'In the event of my not being defended I am completely in the hands of the police!' yelled Adams, who then accused Rolfe of allowing important witnesses to look at him through a window at Romford Police Station prior to him being formally identified.

'The less you say yourself now, the better, for you may perhaps say something which may do you harm', Mr Fry told him in an ominously measured tone.

'I will take your advice, sir', said Adams, momentarily somewhat subdued. He even managed to rein himself in while Alfred Marden was asked by Mr Batchelor whether he had any doubt at all about Adams being the man who fired at Simmons and later at himself. Marden answered: 'I have no doubt at all; I am positive.'

Adams, however, could not resist airing his displeasure on another topic. His wife Charlotte had visited him the previous Saturday and told him about the visit by the police. She also seems to have shown him the press report describing his mother-in-law's glee at the prospect of his execution. Adams was furious at what he called this 'foul calumny . . . holding me up as a monster of iniquity, both at home and abroad'. Mr Fry urged him to drop the subject, saying: 'My man, we cannot go into that here.' After being remanded for a further seven days, Adams returned to the matter of the article, a subject which had clearly touched a nerve.

'This will do you no good,' warned the magistrate as Adams whinged from his railed soapbox. 'It will only bring the case against you more prominently before the public.'

'That is exactly what I want! The public are being grossly prejudiced against me . . . I am simply the victim of police hatred and malice . . . That report is a diabolical, malicious falsehood! Whatever I have been in this world, I was always a man to my wife and family. A diabolical, foul, insidious libel it is! . . . My wife is penniless and breadless and the report that she is provided for [by the police] has, to my knowledge, prevented one or two charitably disposed people from assisting her.'

A week later, on 26 March, James Adams came before the Romford magistrates for the final time. He had received no response from the Home Office to his request for legal assistance, and was described as having 'a very dejected and careworn appearance'. The sewage farm labourers Matthews and Kemp, who, as we have seen, had failed to pick out Adams at the identity parade, were questioned again, and still maintained that they were unable to identify him. Charles Woodcraft, Adams's former neighbour, was shown the overcoat discovered at the scene of the shooting and declared he had seen him wearing it.

'You are positive about it?'

'Yes, it is the same in shape, make and colour.'

Another witness that day was Elizabeth Salmon, who had sold the spectacles case found in the overcoat pocket. She stated that to the best of her belief Adams was the man who had purchased the case, but 'He is altered very much, and I cannot positively swear to him.' Adams stood up to point out that she had not chosen him at the identity parade, but had picked out another man.

Detective Sergeant Rolfe took the stand and reinforced his position as Adams's nemesis by providing evidence linking Adams with both the coat and the spectacles. He told the court that in the previous October, he had seen Adams in the Bell in Brick Lane. Adams had been wearing the spectacles in question in order to read the *Morning Post*. Furthermore, Rolfe stated that in January that year, not long before the murder of Simmons, he had again seen Adams, this time in Webb's public house, Whitechapel Road, accompanied by David Dredge and another man, and wearing that very overcoat. It seems that only now, with Adams and Dredge in custody, was Rolfe able to realize the true identities of the men he had observed in the Bell and Webb's.

Adams continually interrupted, declaring that Mr Batchelor was asking leading questions, and insisted the witnesses should be left to tell their own tale. The exasperated prosecutor despaired: 'I don't know why I am here if not to conduct the examination of the witness!' Eventually Mr Fry announced that Adams would be sent for trial before judge and jury.

As Adams was taken down, he could not resist discharging a final, defiant tirade. 'I am utterly at the mercy of those thirsting for my blood, and have been for years. If that is what you call British humanity and justice, I am getting it!' Four constables dragged the struggling man from the court.

Not all the media were totally hostile to Adams. He must have obtained a modicum of relief from a report of an interview with his mother-in-law. She claimed that, during the eight years Adams had been married to her daughter, 'he had been a good husband, never having had a cross word with his wife'. When asked if she had ever fallen on her knees and thanked God that her daughter would soon be a widow, the lady indignantly denied the allegation. Furthermore, the vexed question of the gunman's height was still being aired in the press. The *Essex Times* commented that:

> It will have been noticed by those who have had the opportunity of seeing the prisoner that his height does not quite correspond with that stated in the official description. The latter was supplied by the unfortunate inspector before his death, and the inconsistency may be accounted for by the fact that on the afternoon in question prisoner was wearing a hard felt hat and a long overcoat. It is probable, too, that he might have been wearing high-heeled boots, all of which would lead one to regard him as being taller than he actually is. On the other hand, the late Inspector's opinion as to the man's height was not the same as entertained of him by constables Marden and Emery, and that was expressed at the time.

As we have seen, the murder of Thomas Simmons had sparked renewed debate about the arming of police officers. In February 1885 the question was debated at the Essex Quarter Sessions. A letter from Major Poyntz, the Chief Constable, was read out. Although he was against the general arming of the police, he felt that officers patrolling certain areas of south-west Essex, bordering some of the most disorderly parts of the metropolis, deserved the same protection as their London colleagues. The men of the Metropolitan force were already issued with firearms when going into situations known to be especially perilous.

The justices agreed. Thomas Kemble, chairman of the Constabulary Committee, was reported in the *Chelmsford Chronicle* as declaring that a few years earlier a policeman's truncheon had been sufficient, 'but now there were innumerable men carrying pistols about, and he was told the other day that in the northern towns these deadly weapons were hung up like strings of larks or strings of sausages and

Newgate Prison in the 1880s, as depicted in the *Illustrated London News*.
Authors' collection

were sold from 3s to 5s each'. London criminals, he declared, 'might come over the border into Essex, and, if interfered with, pot off a constable without the constable being able to defend himself'.

Permission having been granted from the Home Secretary, an order for twenty-two revolvers, at £1 17s 6d each, was placed with Philip Webley & Son for use by the Essex force. The guns would only be given to officers wishing to carry them on night duty, and were to be loaded and unloaded by the officer in charge of the police station. They were to be drawn only in self-defence. *The Times* of 3 November 1885 states that 'A number of officers have already undergone a course of revolver practice at the Romford Butts.'

Meanwhile, David Dredge's barrister Philip Stern had been working hard to have his trial held outside Essex. Stern appeared several times before the Justices of the Queen's Bench, stating that it would be impossible to hold a fair trial in the county. He cited the way in which an angry mob had hurled abuse at Dredge in Romford, the fact that a fund was being raised there for the inspector's widow and children, and the sight of placards posted throughout the county describing Dredge as a 'determined burglar'. Dredge himself submitted a supporting statement in which he claimed that the failure of his hay and straw business had led to him making many enemies in the area, presumably his unpaid creditors.

On Tuesday 21 April the Grand Jury considered the evidence and returned a True Bill for murder against both Dredge and Adams. Stern's arguments that justice would be best served by removing the case had been accepted, and it was announced that, under Palmer's Act, the pair would be tried jointly at the Old Bailey.[13] The great wheels of legal machinery were set in motion to begin the process which would place them upon the most daunting stage in the British judicial system.

10

'Guilty or Not Guilty of Wilful Murder?'

Dredge and Adams were transferred to Newgate Prison to await their trial. Until its demolition in 1902, the forbidding, windowless, granite walls of Newgate scowled down upon the streets of London as, to quote Hepworth Dixon in his *London Prisons*, 'the Bastille once did upon the Rue St Antoine'. During its grisly history thousands of souls passed through Newgate's menacing doors to confront their destiny in the Old Bailey Sessions House – the Central Criminal Court as it became in 1834 – which adjoined the prison.[14] A murder trial at the Old Bailey provided the Victorians with a diversion from workaday drudgery as entertaining and enthralling as anything the music hall or theatre could offer. The electrifying sense of high drama was intensified by the awareness that the lives of the accused were in dire jeopardy. On the morning of Monday 27 April 1885 the stage was set for David Dredge and James Adams. By a strange coincidence, the previous trial, which had ended on Saturday afternoon, had involved a 21-year-old Romford woman named Elizabeth Salmons, sentenced to death for murdering her 2-year-old daughter. (She was, incidentally, no relation to Elizabeth Salmon, wife of the Seymour Street optician.)

Dredge and Adams were brought from their cells and escorted through Dead Man's Walk, the paved, enclosed passageway connecting the prison with the courthouse. They must have shuddered to see, carved into the wall, initial letters of the surnames of executed prisoners lying beneath the flagstones. Awaiting trial, Adams had reportedly been violent and even suicidal. His mood must have lifted to some degree on learning that the court had appointed a barrister, 45-year-old John Peter Grain, to present his defence. Mr Grain, who had been called to the Bar at the Middle Temple in 1873, would be one of the defence team at the trial of Oscar Wilde ten years later. From the moment he entered the dock Adams was engaged in deep conversation with Mr Grain, whom he had not met before. While evidence was being given Adams continually passed notes to him over the rail of the dock. The packed courtroom included tearful friends and family of the accused men.

The Clerk of the Arraigns, Mr Henry Kemp Avory,[15] demanded silence and ordered all to stand for the entrance of the judge, 67-year-old Mr Justice Hawkins, resplendent in wig and scarlet robe. Henry Hawkins had been born in Hitchin, Hertfordshire, and had studied at the Middle Temple before being called to the Bar in 1843. He had been a judge since 1859, and was awarded a knighthood in 1876. He would eventually be raised to the peerage as Baron Brampton of Brampton, and reach the age of 90. Sir Henry had presided over numerous Old Bailey murder trials and had become one of the most popular and well-known judges with the general public who, with its flair for sardonic humour, had dubbed him 'Hanging Hawkins'. This nickname gave an entirely false impression of extreme severity. In reality Sir Henry was a very patient and assiduous judge who took great pains to ensure that defendants were treated with complete impartiality and had every opportunity to make their case. Adams was charged as 'John Lee alias James Lee alias James Manson', and listed on the calendar of prisoners as 45 years old, a baker by trade, who could read and write well. Dredge was listed as a dealer aged 52, who could read and write imperfectly. When the charge was read out, the defendants answered simultaneously 'Not Guilty'.

Two legal giants of the day, Henry Bodkin Poland and Stephen Montagu Williams, had been selected to mount the prosecution. Mr Poland (who later became Sir Henry) had, at that time, lived 56 years of the 99 which he would subsequently attain. He had been called to the Bar at the Inner Temple in 1851 and appointed counsel to the Treasury and Home Office in 1865. According to *Vanity Fair* magazine, Mr Poland 'is better known to the public than any other member of the Bar, for he appears in every sensational case'. He had earned a reputation as a ruthless

NEWGATE—CRIMINALS' BURIAL GROUND

Dead Man's Walk. *From W J Loftie, London City (1891)*

interrogator. In 1881 a *Daily Telegraph* journalist had compared the effect of his entrance into court upon a formerly brash murderer, Percy Lefroy Mapleton, to that which the sight of a mongoose has upon a cobra. 'It was only a quiet, ferret-like creature . . . Yet to the cobra, venomous, deadly as it was, the look of that mongoose was as the sight of death.'

Stephen Montagu Williams, then aged 50, was the son and grandson of barristers and had been educated at Eton. He brought experience of many walks of life to his present calling. He had been, for a time, a classics master at Ipswich Grammar School. He later served in the 41st Regiment of Foot during the Crimean War, and after leaving the army had become an actor in a touring company. Only after his marriage in 1858 did he decide to enter the law. He was called to the Bar of the Inner Temple in 1862, and by 1879 had been appointed junior prosecuting counsel to the Treasury. His career as one of the most acclaimed advocates at the Old Bailey was, sadly, to be cut short in 1886 when an operation for cancer of the throat destroyed his voice, although he continued to serve as a magistrate until his death in 1892.

The first witness for the prosecution was Frederick Wilderspin, who described once more how he had seen three men leave the train at Rainham. James Adams's spirits must have lifted to hear Wilderspin state that 'The man *not* in custody appeared to be the tallest of the three'. Alfred Marden was next

to be called, but contradicted Wilderspin, asserting that he was positive that the third man was shorter than Adams. The jury listened intently while Marden described his ordeal.[16] When Adams's counsel, Mr Grain, began his cross-examination, Marden answered in a clear and self-assured voice. He asserted that, although dusk was falling at the time of the shooting, it was far from dark. He stated that he had been 'just inside the hedge' when the shot was fired, and agreed that

The judge, Sir Henry Hawkins.
Authors' collection

he had previously taken a glass of ale in the Cherry Tree.

Philip Stern stood up to interrogate his old adversary. Inevitably one of his questions was 'What sort of revolver did Dredge have?' Marden, still smarting from their last encounter, was this time fully prepared. Even Stern must have suppressed a smile at the constable's glaringly rehearsed response to his question.

'I cannot give any description of the revolver,' said Marden, stiffly, 'for revolvers are funny things to describe. I know it was a chambered revolver.'

'No wonder you can't, young man!' yelled Dredge from the dock. He had denied all along that he had carried a gun.

Stern continued with a salvo of brisk questioning. 'Have you ever heard anyone say that the hedge is ten feet high at its lowest point?'

'No, I have not'.

'Is not the bank five feet high?'

'No sir, there is no bank there.'

'How far were you from where the Inspector was shot?'

'About 60 yards.'

After a break for lunch, PC George Emery entered the witness box, followed by Ned Matthews, one of the sewage farm labourers. Cross-examined by Mr Grain, Matthews declared he had not heard any shots fired while following Marden in pursuit of the gunmen near the haystacks. If there had been any, he was sure he would have heard them.

As the day wore on, the jury absorbed and digested the evidence. Slowly they began to assemble a picture of the pattern of events from the jumbled fragments of information presented to them. They heard Kemp's account of how David Dredge had stood chatting with him after the shooting. They listened, engrossed, as Sergeant Chase described the items in the pockets of the oft-mentioned overcoat. They handled the padded socks and key-hole saw discovered in the ditch. They also gave their full attention to William Rolfe as he led them through the events surrounding the arrest of David Dredge. Rolfe read out Dredge's own statement, in which he had asserted that he had *not* been in company with Adams and the third man prior to leaving Rainham Railway Station, but had only been showing them the way to Romford.

Rolfe then turned to the arrest of Adams. Mr Grain put it to Rolfe that when Adams had asked for some breakfast, he had replied 'You, you — dog, I would rather shoot you?' Rolfe denied this, and was supported by PC Day. Mr Grain then pressed Rolfe on the question of whether Marden had looked at Adams through a glass door at Romford Police Station before the formal identity parade.

'Two officers were on duty at the door, and one pushed the door open and said

"Marden is coming down the street". I said "Do not let him anywhere near, because this man is here for identification." It was to prevent him from coming.'

At 4.40 pm the trial was adjourned. The first witness the following morning was Edward Baxter, the pawnbroker's assistant who had surreptitiously summoned the police to arrest Adams. Charles Woodcraft, Adams's neighbour at Caistor Park Road in Plaistow, was next to give evidence. He was followed by Elizabeth Salmon, who was questioned by the judge about her failure to identify Adams at the identity parade.

'Did you think he was the man without any hesitation?'

'No, my Lord. If I had seen the prisoner under similar circumstances as when I sold the case, I should, undoubtedly, have been able to identify him.' She now felt 'no doubt that he is the man'.

At that time a person was not allowed to give evidence in their own defence, so it now fell to the barristers representing Dredge and Adams to present their final arguments.[17] Mr Grain called no witnesses, and made no attempt to put forward an alibi for Adams. Instead, he gave a lengthy speech to the jury, telling them that his client was not the man who fired the fatal shot at Inspector Simmons. He admitted that Adams had been at the scene, as Wilderspin and Emery had deposed, but stressed that no one apart from Marden had identified him as the gunman. Mr Grain put it to the jury that, with darkness gathering, was it likely that Marden, some seventy yards away, could see a man's features clearly enough to have no qualms at sending him to the gallows? He emphasized that Matthews, Kemp and Sawkins had been much closer to the scene, and could hear what was said between the inspector and the gunman. None of them had identified Adams. Mr Grain then asked if it were really possible positively to identify an ordinary overcoat which might be worn by any number of people in London? He also made much of the fact that Mrs Salmon had failed to pick out Adams at the identity parade, initially selecting, in fact, an entirely different man.

Philip Stern now rose on behalf of David Dredge. He called Benjamin Boreham, a hay and straw dealer and cab proprietor of Chadwell Heath. Boreham stated that he had had a quantity of hay in a field near Ford Lane, Hornchurch, and that on the Saturday previous to the shooting he had offered Dredge the job of binding it if he would come down sometime during the early part of the following week.

'Did you receive any letter or confirmation from him as to when he would meet you?' asked the judge.

'No, my Lord.'

'Then there was no reason to suppose that he would be there on that day or on any other?'

'No, my Lord.' Dredge now had a feasible excuse for his excursion to the area on the day in question.

Mr Stern's next witness was Edward Thomas Shaw, a carman of Seething Lane in the City of London. Shaw stated that he often drove from Rainham to Romford Market, and had a good knowledge of the road by the sewage farm.

'And did you go to that location last Sunday for the purpose of making certain trials?' asked Stern.

'Yes sir, I did.'

'And will you tell the jury what you discovered?'

'I measured the hedge on top of the bank and found it to be 10 feet high. I also found that it was impossible for anyone standing in the field to see up the road to a point 60 yards away.'

'May I ask how you came to make these trials Mr Shaw?' requested Mr Poland, although he must have been certain of the reply:

'Yes sir. I went down last week with a friend to take the measurements at the request of Mr Dredge's barrister.'

Philip Stern began his closing speech, described as 'long and laboured' by the *Essex Weekly News*, by stating that this was a blatant attempt to rob an innocent man of his life. There was no evidence that Dredge had done or even contemplated doing anything to bring about the murder of Simmons. Dredge, he emphasized, had always denied even carrying a revolver that day, much less pointing one at Marden. Perhaps, declared Stern, Marden had *thought* he heard Dredge make the threat, and his imagination had led him to believe he *saw* an actual weapon.

The case for the defence now over, Mr Poland now stood up to present his final speech for the prosecution. As he described how Mrs Salmon had proved selling the

The prosecuting barrister, Henry Bodkin Poland. *Author's collection*

glasses case to Adams, there was drama when Adams himself rose to his feet and shouted 'It's a lie, sir, she did not say it!' Mr Poland replied 'I do not think the jury will be of the opinion that Mrs Salmon has lied', but Adams would not be silenced. 'She *has* lied', he stormed. 'If God Almighty had said it I would still say that it was a lie! Why should not the truth be spoken?'

The judge intervened, telling Adams 'I really cannot allow you to speak in this way.'

'I am sorry, my Lord,' he replied, 'but it is hard for a man in my position to have his life sworn away by the police. I have witnesses here who will swear that Mrs Salmon picked out a man who is as different from me as I am from a black man!' Mr Justice Hawkins reluctantly allowed Adams to call Walter Thacker, a warder at Chelmsford prison, and put questions to him.

'When did you take charge of me at Chelmsford Prison?'

'On the morning of 11th March.'

'And was I clean shaven with the exception of my moustache?'

'You were.'

'On the 18th March Mrs Salmon came to the prison for the purpose of identifying me. Did I then have any beard?'

'No.'

'Did Mrs Salmon pick out another man?'

'Yes, she did.'

The man chosen from the line-up by Mrs Salmon then entered the court. His name was Balls, and he was seventeen years younger than Adams. The *Chelmsford Chronicle* noted that he was 'a man of about the same height and build as the prisoner, but is decidedly darker and is unlike him in general appearance'. Adams next asked for Mrs Salmon to be recalled, and she was duly brought in to face him.

'When you were asked to identify the man who had bought the eye-glasses case', Adams demanded, transfixing the nervous woman with a steely glare, 'did you not say, "I hardly know but I think that is the man" and picked the man beside me?'

'Yes, because you had altered in appearance. You had a stumpy beard and were looking ill and older.'

Mr Poland intervened, asking Mrs Salmon what her thoughts were now, concerning the identity of the prisoner. She replied, 'I believe he is the man who purchased the spectacles case.'

Mr Poland eventually completed his speech to the jury, and Mr Justice Hawkins began his summing-up. The *Essex Times* reported that 'At this stage, prisoners became more agitated and seemed to realize their critical position more than they had hitherto done.' The judge pointed out that the case against Dredge was considerably different to that against Adams, and stated that, if an application had been made, he might well have ordered separate trials. His Lordship drew the jury's attention to the main pieces of evidence against Adams, namely the overcoat and the spectacles case, and said that in his opinion these had a very important bearing on the case. In Dredge's favour, he said, the evidence for him being party to the affair was 'extremely slight'.

Adams was, of course, determined to have the final word. 'Before the jury retires, I wish to make a statement. It is as to the opportunities that the police had of seeing me before I was placed for identification, and as to the treatment I received from the police from the moment of my arrest until my committal. I was dragged through the streets of Romford on two or three occasions previous to identification. All that Rolfe has said is false. He has pursued me for six or seven years.'

He went on 'You know what I am and the police know what I am, and it is the effect of the police knowing what I am that places me here today . . . I charge Rolfe with downright falsehood and Day with perjury.'

The judge would hear no more. 'I ought not to allow you to go on. I am giving you an indulgence which, if a man was charged with a less serious crime, I should be obliged to refuse. I must tell the jury that they cannot treat your statements as absolute gospel truths just because you have uttered them.'

The jury now retired, and at 7 pm, less than an hour later, they returned, having reached unanimous verdicts. A deep enveloping silence fell upon the courtroom. 'Do you find David Dredge guilty or not guilty of the wilful murder of Thomas Simmons?'

'Not guilty.'

David Dredge was a hard man, but this ordeal had brought him close to the edge of the abyss. He gripped the rail of the dock, buried his face in his handkerchief and sobbed audibly.

The time now came for the verdict on Adams.

'Guilty.'

All eyes now turned towards Adams as the clerk asked him if he had anything to say. True to form, Adams replied: 'Yes, I have. In the first place, the witness Wilderspin said that the tallest man of the three was not present and . . .'

The judge cut him short: 'I cannot allow you now to argue the case over again.'

'I was asked if I had any reasons to give why sentence should not be passed and I was giving them', Adams responded. Some in the public gallery must have been enjoying every moment of this dialogue between dock and bench. Others, Adams's wife and family among them, would surely have blenched at the doomed man's desperate petitions which, once the jury had declared their verdict, could in no way avert the sentence which must soon be passed.

'I have told you', explained Mr Justice Hawkins, 'that you cannot now disturb the verdict of the jury. Even if you were to satisfy me that the jury were wrong I could not now interfere with their finding.' Newspaper reporters present in the court were scribbling frantically as Adams, determined to go down fighting, persisted with his impossible cause. 'Then what is the point of my saying anything? The meaning of the formal address to me is nothing more than a farce!'

'This is not a moment for trifling', admonished the judge.

'This is no trifling matter to me, my Lord, if it is for you. I am speaking as a persecuted and judicially murdered man. I have nothing more to say, my Lord. Do your duty.'

The black cap, the rolled square of black silk which had been lying on the bench throughout the proceedings, was now placed upon the judge's wig. 'The crime you have been found guilty of is that of having wilfully murdered Inspector Simmons . . .'

Adams interrupted the judge with a cry of 'I *did not* do it!'

'I believe you are *not* a persecuted man. I believe you have had as much justice done to you as any man in this country . . . I believe their verdict is the right one.' The judge then passed the chilling sentence of death, his grim words punctuated by the sound of a woman sobbing in the public gallery. 'You will be taken to the place from whence you came, and from thence to the place of execution, and that you there be hanged by the neck until you are dead, and that your body be afterwards buried within the precincts of the gaol in which you shall be last confined after your conviction; and may the Lord have mercy on your soul.' Adams, defiant to the end, roared from the dock: 'I have had none from the judge, nor justice neither!'

The jury foreman added that they wished to compliment Alfred Marden upon his bravery, and the manner in which he had given his evidence. His Lordship said he heartily agreed with them. If David Dredge had thought his ordeal was now over, he was mistaken. Mr Montagu Williams reminded the judge that there was still an outstanding charge against Dredge of threatening Marden with a revolver, and Dredge was immediately rearrested. The time was nearing 8 pm. The judge made his exit, legal staff gathered together their papers, and the spectators left the public gallery. As the players departed the stage was left empty, and the theatre of justice fell silent.

Adams was allowed a few words of farewell with Charlotte and his children. He was then taken in a prison van to Liverpool Street Station, handcuffed and escorted by six prison officers armed with swords, and put on the 8.40 pm mail train to Chelmsford. At stations along the route, including Romford, people clustered around the compartment in which Adams sat, but the blinds were tightly drawn so that he could not be seen. More crowds gathered at Chelmsford Station, but police and railway officials stopped them from reaching the platform. When the train steamed in at 9.50 pm, Adams was whisked down the station stairs and placed in a fly for the final leg of his journey.

In prison, Adams exhibited broad mood-swings, fluctuating between deep, silent depression and impassioned outbursts avowing his innocence and the flaws of the judicial system. The *Chelmsford Chronicle* told its readers that he 'was the most unmanageable prisoner who had occupied the condemned cell within the memory of the oldest official at the prison'. The cell was much larger than all the others, and two warders remained with Adams around the clock. This was normal practice preceding an execution, but a particularly close watch was kept on Adams. He was judged a suicide risk, having apparently claimed that 'there was not the man living and there was not the rope made that could hang him'. He took regular exercise in the prison yard, but no other inmates were allowed there at the same time.

On the morning of Friday 1 May (his forty-first birthday, according to the information in his convict licence of 1877) Adams was visited by the high sheriff of Essex, Joseph F Lescher, who told him that the execution had been fixed for Monday, 18 May. Adams reportedly received the news calmly, stating that he did not fear death on his own account, but was anxious about the destitute condition of his wife and children. The press overwhelmingly backed the verdict. The *Telegraph*, for example, vilified him as 'one of those tameless, desperate, implacable ruffians against whom society must wage a war of extermination'.

Adams's wife Charlotte, on the other hand, was widely pitied. On the afternoon of 2 May, the Saturday following the verdict, she made her way to the prison. The visiting area was inside the Porter's Lodge. Prisoners and visitors were kept about four feet apart, separated by a passageway with a grating in each wall. They had no privacy, a warder being stationed in the passage between them. Charlotte was to tell the press that 'I was four and a half hours in the place before I could see him or get him into a state to see me.' When Adams eventually appeared, the pair spent about an hour in conversation. Charlotte was then offered refreshment at a nearby cottage. Springfield residents had also collected clothing and food for her and her family.

Two days later, other family members arrived asking to see Adams, as he related in a letter to his wife. 'I saw your brother John and my sister and her husband, and my mother also came; but I persuaded my brother and sister not to let her come and visit me this time, as it would have been too terrible an ordeal even for me – a strong man. How much more so for my poor mother at 83 years of age?'

The visitors had been drinking at various public houses in Springfield throughout the day, and Adams's sister sported a black eye. Their interview with Adams was most distressing, the sound of hysterical wailing resounding throughout the vaulted passageways of the prison. The group's departure at about five o'clock must have been a great relief to the warders. They spent the night in lodgings in Moulsham, newspapers noting that their stay was marked by drunkenness and quarrelling.

Meanwhile, the Under Sheriff had received two letters from a Mrs Sarah Lee, of Walcot, Bath, who had read the condemned man's description in the newspapers and believed him to be her husband, George Lee, a blacksmith. He had, it seems, abandoned her and their six children about five years previously. She stated that he had formerly been a Sunday School teacher, but had taken to drink and got into bad company. It seemed that he had occasionally gone by the name of Adams. The authorities investigated Sarah Lee's claim, but found no evidence to support it. They did concede, however, the possibility that the two men had been partners in crime, and had swapped identities from time to time.

On Thursday, 7 May, three more people applied to visit Adams. They gave their names as William and Mary Brookes, cousins of Adams, from Warren Street near Tottenham Court Road, and William Webster of Chalk Farm. The Brookes were possibly the two witnesses at Adams's wedding. They appeared more respectable than Monday's group, but despite their apparent worthiness were denied admission, the authorities perhaps fearing a repetition of the previous fiasco.

The *Essex Weekly News* reported the strange case of a lofty figure who throughout the week 'has been hovering about the Gaol'. Was he, people wondered, 'the veritable "tall" man wanted . . . drawn here by an irresistible infatuation, in the hope of framing some excuse for obtaining an interview with the condemned man in his cell'. Plain clothes police officers questioned him, but alas 'it was found that there were not sufficient grounds for arresting him on suspicion of being the man who was wanted'.

II

'I Die an Innocent Man. Remember That!'

On the afternoon of Saturday, 9 May Adams's wife paid her second visit to the prison. She saw him for about an hour, and found him 'much more composed' than before. This was not surprising, as he was now aware that support was building on his behalf. Joseph Beaumont, a Coggeshall solicitor, had studied the trial depositions and had agreed to spearhead a campaign to overturn the conviction. The Court of Appeal was not to be established until 1907, and, therefore, the only course of action was to petition the Home Secretary, Sir William Harcourt. The previous Tuesday, 5 May, Beaumont had spent about two hours talking to Adams before composing a formal letter to the Home Office.

Joseph Beaumont was in his fifties and had risen from relatively humble origins as the son of a Colchester baker. He set out his thoughts on the case in a letter published on 8 May in the *Essex Chronicle*:

> I have come to the conclusion that Lee is not guilty of wilful murder and that his case is pre-eminently one for further consideration . . . [He] admits himself to being a burglar and a criminal of a bad type, claiming only that he has been true to his wife and family, and that he is no murderer. He complains loudly, and, I think, not without reason, that being without means, and having no friends, beyond an impecunious wife, he could not supply his counsel with the necessary material for his defence.

Beaumont then drew attention to the discrepancy of height between Adams, only 5 feet 8 inches, and the gunman described by both Simmons and Marden as 6 feet. Was it not possible, argued Beaumont, that when the third man was caught he might turn out to be the 6-footer? He criticized the depositions as 'meagre and inconsistent', and concluded: 'Indignation against the murderer of Simmons is justly great but we must be careful not to shock society by allowing that indignation to blind us, so that we hang the wrong man.'

A flurry of letters and editorial comment on the subject of Adams occupied newspaper columns for several weeks. On 15 May a letter signed 'Justice' was published in the *Essex Chronicle*, supporting Mr Beaumont's argument: 'The police placard, issued, remember, just after the occurrence, describes [the murderer] as six feet high, stout build, 33 years of age.' The writer also made the more controversial point that 'Up to that time there was no overt act committed by the prisoners which justified Simmons in arresting or searching them. The crime is therefore clearly manslaughter and not murder. There is no doubt that the police in this county are an able, intelligent body of men, nor that Simmons was an excellent officer; but it seems equally clear that he fell a victim to an excess of zeal on his part.'

On the other hand, an *Essex Chronicle* editorial dismissed Mr Beaumont's arguments as being 'totally without foundation . . . so far as we know, there has rarely been more satisfactory evidence of the guilt of a prisoner in a case of the same nature'. A lengthy letter by Benjamin Baker of Brentwood supported this view, stating that Marden's identification of Adams could be relied upon because he had had five separate opportunities to see the face of the gunman.

On Tuesday 12 May, three days after his wife's visit, Adams sat down to pen a six-page letter to her in his large, straggling hand. It was later printed in the *Essex Weekly News*. 'My dear', he began, 'when I picture to myself the misery and disgrace I have brought on you and my poor children, it nearly drives me mad.' Yet this was not followed by a confession, but by renewed protestations of persecuted innocence: 'when I look upon your poor careworn and anxious face, it causes me to think of the brutal and unjust scoundrels who have literally torn my life from me, and from you and my poor darling children'.

Adams was optimistic that the campaign on his behalf would succeed:

> the gentlemen who have taken up my case have undertaken to see that justice is done to me, and I have the greatest confidence in them, or I should not be waiting as patiently as I am doing, if I seriously thought otherwise except for a moment. My poor soul! I have heard nothing up to the present as to the results of their exertions, but I am confidently waiting, knowing that if the endeavours of these gentlemen are of no avail to procure me justice they will, I am sure, procure for me a respite, that I may lay my case before the country and be heard in my own defence, which defence I have been denied the right of laying before my countrymen, when I know that I should be able to prove my innocence and expose the guilt of my British persecutors. That is all I ask of my country – justice pure and simple.

He ended with eloquent words of affection:

> My poor dear, I do not wish to distress you by asking you to come and see me, as it is no comfort to see you under such unhappy circumstances . . . My dear

wife, I am in the best of health at present, and I hope and trust this will find you and my poor children, not forgetting your mother, brother, and sister, and her husband, the same. Accept my love for yourself and the children, with kisses for all of them . . .

I remain, your loving husband, James Manson.

Meanwhile, the Home Secretary was pondering his decision. Two days later, on 14 May, a letter was sent to Mr Beaumont informing him that the Minister 'has been unable to find any sufficient grounds to justify him in advising interference with the due course of the law'. Mr Beaumont dashed to the Home Office the following day to urge a reconsideration, but to no avail. Adams, who had professed himself to be a Catholic, had received regular visits from 60-year-old Father Charles Batt, minister of the Catholic Church in New London Road, Chelmsford. On the morning of Saturday 16 May, it fell to Father Batt to give Adams the news. The *Chelmsford Chronicle* told its readers that Adams then 'began to rave in a shocking manner and continued shouting until he was quite exhausted'.

That afternoon Charlotte, dressed in black, passed through the heavily studded entrance door of the prison once more. She was accompanied by her

A prison visit, seen from the point of view of the visitor (on the left) and the prisoner (on the right). A prison officer stands between them. *From Henry Mayhew, London Labour and the London Poor (1861), vol. 4*

sister, carrying a baby. Charlotte begged the Governor, Major Henry Eyre Wyatt Lane, to be allowed to see her husband in private. 'This being the last time that I should ever see him, I thought I might have seen him alone.' She was told, however, that the Home Secretary was firm on this point, so the couple were once more separated by the grating. Charlotte's sister remembered that 'The warders did not leave him; they stood behind him. We could scarcely see his face, it was so dark where he was standing. If they had only allowed him to have kissed her through the wirework he should not have done much harm, could he?'

Adams was pleased to hear that his daughter Katey was recovering after being admitted to hospital with a foot complaint. He told Charlotte 'not to part with the children, as he should not like anyone else to have them', and she promised 'I wouldn't let his children go from me'. He raged against the press coverage: 'Whatever they have said in the newspapers against me or my career is false, for I have never uttered a word about my career to anyone; and whatever they have stated they have stated on their own authority.'

When it was time for them, to leave, the women waited in the courtyard in the hope of seeing Adams escorted across it towards his cell. They were to be disappointed, however. Rain was falling, and the warders took Adams back by a different route. Adams had told his wife to go immediately to Mr Charles Gepp, the Under Sheriff of Essex, and Father Batt, and ask them to obtain a week's respite, during which time he said he could prove his innocence. Charlotte accordingly visited Mr Gepp at nearby Upper Terrace, Springfield. We are told that he 'received the poor woman in a most kindly manner, but told her that, although she had done quite right in carrying out her husband's request, he was afraid the respite could not now be granted'.

Later that afternoon Charlotte was interviewed by an *Essex Weekly News* reporter, who wrote that 'from every appearance [she] is a very respectable and well-disposed person'. Asked to describe her husband, she had said that 'Whatever he did beforehand was a mystery to me; but he was always a kind and good husband and a good father . . . What hurt him most was that he could not shake hands with me.'

'Is it true that you told the police that your husband had been cruel to you, and that your mother thanked God that he was out of the way?'

'It is utterly untrue. I could not say that, for he has been the kindest of husbands to me. He has never been cruel to me, nor came home the worse for drink, or anything of that sort. . . . He speaks well of everyone here, and says he must thank them all. They seem very kind to him, and now he wishes he had been tried here.'

Charlotte admitted that at the Old Bailey Adams 'spoke more than he ought to have done . . . raved and tore dreadfully, poor fellow. My poor feelings were bad enough, but what must have been his feelings?' She complained that 'I have his mother living with me, but none of his family have sent me a kind word.' She declared that 'My intention is to try to get sufficient money to buy a mangle, by which I hope I should earn enough to keep my children at school, and get a living for myself and them. The only other means would be to go to service again, if my mother could keep the children, but I am now 40 years of age.'

Charlotte left Chelmsford on the 7.40 pm train, carrying food and clothing donated by the kind-hearted Springfield villagers who had once more given her tea after her gruelling visit to the prison. She had been given some of Adams's belongings, and the reporter noted that 'the one she appeared to value most was the shirt she sent him to wear at his trial'.

Four hours earlier the hangman, James Berry, had stepped off a train at the same station after travelling from his home in Bradford, Yorkshire. Berry, a 33-year-old former policeman, was described by the *Essex Weekly News* as having 'an agreeable appearance for one engaged in such a ghastly occupation; and a not unpleasant style of conversation. His short whiskers are of a gingery hue, and his features are somewhat disfigured by a long scar running from the right eye towards the ear.' The *Essex Times* stated that Berry had 'a sleek and perfectly contented appearance'. He was reported as assuring condemned persons that 'the operation is nothing to be timid about: it is just like the prick of a pin'.

Berry stepped inside the prison and made his way to the exercise yard to the left of the entrance. At the end nearest to Gaol Lane stone steps led down to a pit, 12 feet deep, above which the scaffold had already been erected. It had last been used eight years before, to execute 25-year-old Charles Joseph Revell for killing his wife Esther in Epping Forest. The yard was open to the elements, and a canvas awning had been put over the scaffold to keep the rain off. As we have seen, a man named John Lee had been reprieved earlier that year after the trapdoor failed to open. Believing this was because the woodwork of the scaffold had warped due to the ingress of rainwater, the authorities were anxious to avoid a repeat performance with his namesake.

Berry soon got to work testing the drop and trap using a dummy made of sandbags and matching Adams's height and weight. The aim was to 'give enough rope' so that the condemned man would die instantly rather than be slowly strangled. Unfortunately, as the *Essex Weekly News* reported, Berry's first attempt 'proved if anything rather too effective, for the head of the dummy was snatched off by the fall, and the body with its contents tumbled to the bottom of the pit'. Having eventually satisfied himself that all would go to plan on this occasion, Berry spent Saturday night at the Three Cups in Springfield Road. He was at his leisure all day Sunday, then settled into bed in the debtors' wing of the prison.

Adams, meanwhile, managed a few hours of fitful sleep during his final night, then ate breakfast at 6 am. He seemed impatient to get the dreadful business over and done with. Father Batt arrived shortly before 7 am, but Adams again refused to make confession and be given Holy Communion, maintaining that he was innocent of the crime. During his imprisonment he had kept silent on the subject of the shooting and the fugitive third man.

At 7.50 am the prison bell began to toll. Earlier that morning James Berry had again tested the mechanical workings of the scaffold. He now strolled up and down the yard carrying the leather straps which he would use to pinion Adams's arms. Five press reporters had been admitted, and Berry explained to them that the rope was 5/8ths of an inch in diameter, and that he had so far carried out nineteen hangings using that rope and another, dividing the work fairly between them. An assistant of Berry's at a later execution explained the process to the

Carlisle Patriot newspaper. 'The noose is formed by passing an end of the rope through a brass eye, and is kept in position by a small leather loop which runs along the rope . . . The brass eye of the noose was fixed just under the left ear, because, apart from the dislocation of the neck, there were two arteries which the knot caused to burst, and which of themselves were enough to cause death.'

This image of Adams alias Lee may depict his wax effigy in Madame Tussaud's. *Essex Police Museum*

At two or three minutes before 8 am Berry entered Adams's cell to pinion his arms. This was done by fastening a strap two inches wide around his waist, to which were attached two wristlets of leather. These kept Adams's hands in such a position that the tips of the fingers of both hands just touched at the front. A single strap was then passed inside the elbows at the back, and fastened securely, thus forcing him to stand upright. Adams submitted without a struggle, but continued his vocal complaints. He inveighed against the Home Secretary for not allowing his wife to shake hands with him. He declared that he was not being hung for the murder of Inspector Simmons but for his previous crimes. Adams was then escorted from the cell, extra warders in attendance because of his reputation for violence. The procession was headed by the Sheriff's Marshal, Mr Powell, ceremonially carrying his staff of office. Behind Adams walked Sir Claude Champion de Crespigny, an Essex baronet and magistrate. Others in the party included the prison governor Major Lane, Walter Gepp acting Under Sheriff, Father Batt and Reverend Lumley the prison chaplain.

The *Essex Weekly News* reporter was impressed by the condemned man's courage, writing that his appearance was 'undaunted and resolute . . . His face was deadly pale, but he walked quickly and firmly, almost outstripping the warders. He gave a hurried glance at the representatives of the Press, and then at the engine of death, towards which he promptly made his way and took his stand upon the trap doors just under the rope.'

As Berry busied himself in strapping his legs Adams said: 'I thank you all, gentlemen, for your kindness that I have received in this prison.' The white hood was drawn over his head, and from beneath it came a broken voice with the heart-rending cry of 'Oh my poor wife and children!' Then, as Berry prepared to draw the bolt, Adams made a final protestation, 'in firm, even fierce tones', according to the *Essex Times* reporter.

'I die an innocent man', he proclaimed. 'Remember that!'

No sooner had the words left his lips than the trapdoor opened and Adams plunged from view. Berry had administered a drop of 8 feet 6 inches. Although the rope quivered for a minute or two, it seemed that death had occurred instantaneously.

Nearly 300 people had gathered outside on Springfield Hill. The crowd was small compared with the thousands who had flocked there in the days when hangings took place in full view on top of the gatehouse. Police officers patrolled to prevent anyone climbing the prison wall or up the tall trees. As 8 am approached, people could hear the tolling of the chapel bell within the prison walls. All eyes turned to the flagpole over the governor's office, and when the black flag was hoisted just after 8 am a visible shudder passed through the crowd. Inside, the official party withdrew leaving the broken body of the transgressor hanging for an hour in the pit. It was then taken down and placed in a coffin ready for the inquest. Usually it was a basic pine coffin roughly constructed within the prison, but in this case a casket of better quality had been provided by a local undertaker. After a brief inquest, the body of Adams was buried near the east wall of the prison, abutting onto Gaol Lane, near others who had shared his fate.

Looking back at the whole tale, the *Chelmsford Chronicle* declared that 'the credit of bringing to justice one who had for so many years been at war with society is almost entirely due to Rolfe'. It stressed that the detective had knowingly put his own life at risk in the pursuit, and noted approvingly that 'the Commissioners of Police have, we understand, marked their sense of his conduct by a reward'. This testimonial was accompanied by the Number I Certificate. Adams was to receive a different sort of recognition. Ken Frost, in his essay on the case for the *Romford Record* magazine in 1986, notes that a wax effigy of him 'was placed in Tussaud's Chamber of Horrors exhibition where it remained until 1968'.

On 26 May 1885 the appeal on behalf of Mary Ann Simmons and her children was formally closed. The Essex Chief Constable, Major Poyntz, announced that an impressive total of £1,048 13s had been raised. Similar efforts were being made for the widow and family of the man hanged for the crime. A letter in the *Chelmsford Chronicle* made this plea:

> Putting aside her last sorrows, she is left with her young family (the baby only three months old and very ill) alone to care and provide for them. Will not some of those who have given so liberally to the widow of the late Inspector Simmons think also of this poor deserving woman, who is left in shame, sorrow and need?

Two months later, in July 1885, David Dredge entered the dock at the Essex Assizes at Chelmsford. The main charge was of assaulting Alfred Marden, and he was also accused of assault with intent to resist the arrest of himself, Adams and the third man. The prosecuting barrister, Mr Forrest Fulton (later Sir Forrest Fulton, QC) called Marden, who again stated that Dredge had pointed a revolver at him and shouted 'You ——. I'll blow your —— brains out with this'. PC Wilderspin once more described watching the three men leave the train at Rainham. For the defence, Philip Stern contended that Marden, being in 'a state of excitement at the time', had made a mistake, and that Dredge had not been carrying a revolver. He called as a witness David Kemp, who described how Dredge had waited with him by the police horse and trap for more than fifteen minutes before walking away.

The jury, however, returned a verdict of guilty. Stern then reminded the judge that Dredge had been in prison on remand since February, 'and had been placed in much suspense by his trial for murder'. Dredge yelled from the dock: 'I never had a revolver in my hand in my life. If I lay on my dying bed now I would say so.'

Stern then called Detective Sergeant Rolfe into the witness box for the defence. Rolfe had previously described the actual arrest of Dredge. He now told the court that Dredge had been in steady employment for some years, and had been given a good character by his employers. He had, however, suffered unemployment for five months before the attack on Simmons and as a result had fallen into the orbit of Adams.

The judge, John Walter Huddleston (styled Baron Huddleston) stated his belief that the verdict was the right one. Dredge, he declared, was 'an habitual criminal, probably regardless of truth and with a certain amount of cunning'.

'I beg your pardon; I never knowed the men,' interrupted Dredge. He stated that he had nothing against Simmons – quite the contrary, for the inspector had treated

A prisoner undergoing hard labour. He was required to turn the crank handle thousands of times a day. *From Henry Mayhew, London Labour and the London Poor (1861), vol. 4*

him to a bottle of ginger-beer the last time they met, and urged him to 'mind he went on all right'. Dredge went on to protest that he was 'as innocent as a child . . . this was a scandalous and rascally shame'. He alleged that Marden 'had tried to swear his life away, and now he was trying to swear his liberty away'.

The judge announced that Dredge's assertions made no impression upon him, as he found the evidence to be 'perfectly convincing'. He began reading out Dredge's lengthy list of previous convictions. When he came to a poaching offence from February 1863, Dredge interrupted with 'I was fined 28s 6d for shooting a partridge!' at which the spectators burst out laughing. Eventually the judge pronounced a sentence of twelve months' imprisonment with hard labour.

'I humbly beg your pardon, my Lord, but I am going to do this 12 months as innocent as a child', protested Dredge. Pointing to Superintendent Dobson, he shouted 'He is the only man I have got to thank for this!' The sting of resentment must surely, though, have been tempered by the awareness that had matters taken a different turn, he would have walked alongside Adams to the scaffold.

Summer turned into autumn, and Dobson, Rolfe and Mellish must have feared that there was by now little likelihood of capturing the third participant in the Simmons case. Yet forces were even then at work which would bring the episode to its gripping finale, two hundred miles away in the far north of England.

12

'Smeared with the Blood of their Victim'

William Rolfe was certainly not the man to rest content with two out of three, though he had relatively little to go on relating to the identity of the final fugitive. With Dredge there had been a name and a photograph, and the search for Adams had been boosted by the label inside the glasses case. Now that he had met Adams and Dredge in person, Rolfe broadened the search to encompass criminal associates they had in common. One name came to the fore – that of John White, who used the alias John Martin. Rolfe was convinced that in the weeks leading up to the shooting of Simmons, White/Martin had been a regular drinking companion of both Adams and Dredge inside Webb's, near the junction of Whitechapel High Street and Commercial Street.

Rolfe and his colleagues launched an immediate hunt for Martin, but he seemed to have disappeared from his usual East End haunts. One morning in August 1885, however, three months after the execution of Adams, their quarry was tempted to risk a stroll along the Commercial Road. Among the crowds the sudden sound of a well-known rolling Wiltshire accent must have stung him to the quick.

'White, I want you!'

The man turned, and Rolfe must have thought he was within a few feet of closing the file on the case that had dominated his waking thoughts since January. However, luck was to desert him this time. Martin thrust his hand ostentatiously into his jacket pocket.

'Take a step closer and I'll put a bullet through your eye!'

Rolfe dared not take the chance that Martin was bluffing. His previous record indicated that it was more than likely that he did carry a gun. With a derisive grin Martin turned away and disappeared into the maze of side streets, leaving Rolfe to contemplate his missed opportunity.

Martin was around 40 years of age, and had a long face, dark brown hair and moustache, and short side-whiskers. His distinguishing feature was a large wart or mole between his eyes. He was a taciturn individual who gave away very little about his background to anyone, least of all to the police. He claimed to be a cigar maker by trade, born in County Cork, Ireland. He later stated that he nursed bitter memories of his first brush with prison life, when at the age of 14 he had endured two weeks in London's notorious Newgate Prison. This punishment, he declared, had led him 'by degrees from bad to worse'.

A close search of the Newgate registers reveals only one John White (as we have seen, this was Martin's real name) who fits the bill: a 15-year-old from Bishopsgate in the City of London, imprisoned in 1860 for stealing a watch. After two weeks in Newgate, he had served most of the remainder of his twelve-month sentence at Parkhurst Prison on the Isle of Wight. A clinching piece of evidence, surely, is that this John White also had a mole between his eyes. He too had connections with County Cork, as it was the birthplace of his father Maurice (or Morris) White, a tailor. Young John had formerly worked with his father 'on the knocker' – that is, buying second-hand clothing by calling door-to-door then refurbishing it for resale. On completing his sentence he seems to have given up any attempt at honest employment.

Released from one spell of imprisonment in 1883, White/Martin was almost immediately reconvicted and served a further two terms of six months each in close succession. He could not have long been free from his last period of custody when the murder of Simmons took place. Around September 1885, soon after this confrontation with Rolfe, Martin was approached by two fellow criminals who asked him to travel with them to the North of England and Scotland, making use of the railway network to seek out targets for burglary. Their names were Anthony Benjamin Rudge and James Baker.

The origins of Rudge, like those of Martin, are obscured by his habit of using aliases and also falsifying his age and place of birth. He would later claim to originate from Bolton in Lancashire but, like Martin, he was actually a Londoner. He had been born William Fennell on 12 December 1845 at 18 Half Nichol Street, Bethnal Green, in the heart of an area called the Old Nichol.[18] This was one of the most deprived neighbourhoods of London, and would be graphically depicted in 1896 by Arthur Morrison in his novel *A Child of the Jago*. His parents were John Fennell, a dustman, and his wife Catherine (nee Britt), both originally from Ireland. They had married in 1843 and had two other surviving children, Hannah (two years older than William) and Thomas (nine years younger).

John Fennell's cousin Thomas Walsh was living with the family at the time of the 1851 census. By 1861 John Fennell had died, and the widowed Catherine later married Thomas Walsh.

The *Carlisle Journal* stated that Rudge had been brought up by his grandfather. It related that 'he was still young when he began to frequent racecourses, gamble and live by his wits; and then step by step he sank into those lower depths of crime which he has now drained to the dregs'. Rudge later claimed to have lived in Texas, where, he declared, 'every boy carries a revolver', but this claim has not been substantiated. In November 1870 Rudge was convicted at the Clerkenwell Sessions of housebreaking, and sentenced to five years' penal servitude. He is recorded on the 1871 census at Pentonville Prison as William Fennell, born at Bethnal Green, cook, aged 25 and married. He spent most of his sentence in the stone quarries at Portland alongside James Adams and David Dredge.

Released in November 1874, Rudge rather foolishly attempted ten months later to break into a house at Edmonton at 7.30 in the evening when the occupants were at home. He was soon captured, but determined to escape at all costs he somehow managed to squeeze through the window of a cab taking him to Newgate. Luckily for the police a passer-by was carrying a hammer, and obeyed a call to strike the fugitive on the head with it. Rudge duly appeared at the Old Bailey in October 1875 and was found guilty of housebreaking. In an attempt to conceal his previous conviction he had taken five years off his age and given his name as William Walsh (Walsh being, as we have seen, the name of his stepfather). This subterfuge did not succeed, however, and the judge levied the savage sentence of ten years' penal servitude in return for the pathetic haul of a coat and a bag of school books.

A prison photograph taken of Rudge in 1876 shows a man with a round face, bulging forehead and an alert expression. This time round, his years of labouring on 'the Public Works' were spent not at Portland but further east along the south coast at Portsea Convict Prison, built in 1852 to replace the prison hulks that had formerly floated in

Anthony Benjamin Rudge, photographed in Pentonville Prison in 1876 under of the name of William Walsh. *The National Archives*

Portsmouth Harbour. In the 1881 census he was listed as William Walsh, a stoker, married, and born in London. His age was given as 31 (as we have seen, he was actually five years older than this). Eventually, in 1884, Rudge emerged from this period of incarceration, which he afterwards described as a 'living death', a bitter and vicious man. He had now spent at least a third of his 39 years behind bars.

By 1885 Rudge had grown rather stout, and his brown hair was thinning on top. Like James Adams he had made the most of the educational opportunities offered by the convict system. He was a great reader, and could hold forth about works as varied as Milton's *Paradise Lost* and Edgar Allen Poe's *Tales of Mystery and Imagination*. He spoke so well that according to the *Carlisle Journal* he gained a reputation as 'a sort of thieves' orator, – "the Attorney General of the Thieves' Confederacy" he is called – and his style is that of a man accustomed to low mob oratory'.

James Baker, at 29, was the youngest of the group, and also hailed from the notorious Old Nichol in Bethnal Green. Known as Jimmy, he was the third child of Thomas Baker, a blacksmith later turned furniture dealer, and his wife Ellen (or Elender) Blumson, who had married in 1852. He had been born on 29 November 1856 at 17 Old Castle Street, his mother's family home, and brought up at Virginia Row.

Jimmy was only 19 when he married 18-year-old Eliza Harriet Bostock at St Matthew's Church, Bethnal Green, on 5 August 1876. The newlyweds lived for two months above an undertaker's shop in the Hackney Road before moving in with Eliza's parents William and Alice Bostock above their general store at 16 Margaret Place, Bethnal Green. Baker had been brought up to the family trade of furniture-making but had decided to follow, like James Adams, the career of an accomplished 'ladder and portico thief'. Baker had extraordinary agility and athletic prowess in scaling buildings which even earned him the grudging admiration of the police.

Things had gone wrong for young Jimmy, however, on 23 November 1876, only three months after his marriage. He was helping himself to jewellery and other valuables from the bedroom of a solicitor named Edwin Howard at Silverdale House in Lewisham when the alarm was raised. Baker fell when trying to make a quick exit through the window, and suffered a broken arm and head injuries. He made his way back home, but was arrested a few days later and subsequently sentenced to five years' penal servitude.

Baker was given a ticket of leave in 1881, but was caught pickpocketing shortly afterwards and sent back to prison. 'Going straight' was easier said than done. As Thomas Archer wrote in *The Pauper, the Thief and the Convict* in 1865: 'In this

Two prison photographs of James Baker, taken (left) in 1877 and (right) in 1881.
The National Archives

country, and especially in London, a discharged convict has very little chance of obtaining honest employment by which he can live comfortably; or of keeping it even when he has obtained it, after his antecedents once become known.' Baker would later serve other, shorter, spells behind bars.

According to the *Carlisle Journal*, Baker was 'rather below the middle height, of slender build, with very black curly hair, and a black moustache'. It speculated that he had 'apparently foreign blood in his veins – possibly he is of Gypsy extraction' and another newspaper stated that he 'has an unmistakeable Italian physiognomy'.

Baker's wife Eliza had deserted him during his first spell in prison. He afterwards met a girl named Nellie at Carlisle Races and brought her back to London to live with him. Nellie's full name is currently unknown, but she was apparently from the north of England, born in Manchester and brought up in Carlisle, Cumberland. The couple settled down to run a greengrocer and general provisions shop in Montague Street in Baker's native Bethnal Green. Notwithstanding this legitimate 'front', young Jimmy still continued his criminal activities. The *Carlisle Journal* later declared that 'if Baker's history could be written it would disclose some extraordinary adventures on the Continent as well as in this country . . . His way of dealing with the jewels he stole was to take out the precious stones and sell them in the ordinary market for such commodities, and then melt the gold settings.'

Having considered the proposal of Rudge and Baker in that autumn of 1885, John Martin may have been only too ready to grab the chance of escaping the unwelcome attention of the Whitechapel CID and pocket some much-needed cash into the bargain. A *Carlisle Patriot* journalist noted that 'Their perverted talents were variously adapted for the work – Rudge being a bold and enterprising character, capable of planning and leading, while Martin was a reliable lieutenant, and Baker, though lacking courage, was nimble and adroit.'

The expedition did not begin well for the trio. Robbery attempts at Newcastle, Liverpool, Glasgow, Edinburgh and other places either failed altogether or netted small returns. The men's sights then turned towards the county of Cumberland. The annual Border Union Hare Coursing Meet, lasting several days, was about to take place on land belonging to baronet Sir Frederick Ulric Graham of Netherby Hall near Longtown. (Coursing is an ancient blood sport in which greyhounds compete to catch hares over a measured distance.) Rudge, Martin and Baker travelled by rail from Edinburgh to Carlisle on Saturday 24 October 1885. Approaching the end of the journey, their interest was stirred by the splendid appearance of Netherby Hall itself, standing amongst the distant trees. It was described in Kelly's 1894 *Directory of Cumberland and Westmorland* as 'a mansion of red brick in the Italian style' chiefly dating from the eighteenth century.

On Tuesday 27 October Rudge, Martin and Baker took an excursion train from Carlisle to Gretna provided for patrons of the first day of the coursing meet. Arriving just after 9 am, they left three large black leather portmanteaus at the office of the station-master, Alexander Maclean, before proceeding to the event. John Martin was a familiar figure at racing and coursing meetings as a runner for betting men between the circuit and the telegraph office. According to the *Carlisle Journal*, he was recognized that day by a Lord Haddington, who spoke to him. Martin complained that there was not much doing in his line of business that day.

At 3 pm the following afternoon, Wednesday, Baker entered Gretna Railway Station, reclaimed one of the bags and took it across the green into the Graham Arms. The innkeeper's son-in-law, David Johnstone, showed them into a public room off the entrance hall. Having the room to themselves, Baker and his companions opened the bag and removed one of several bunches of keys. A key was taken from this, heated in the fire, manipulated and finally cooled in a glass of rum. The men had, however, reckoned without Johnstone, who had never liked the look of these flashy 'sporting gentlemen' and was at that very moment watching their every movement through a crack in the door. Johnstone shot straight to the kitchen to spread the news that there were thieves in the house. When he returned Rudge, Martin and Baker had vanished. They had set off along the road in the direction of Longtown, having left their luggage at the station with instructions to forward it to Carlisle, labelled 'A. Smith – To be called for.'

That evening, two miles away at Netherby Hall, Sir Frederick Graham and his wife Lady Jane Hermione (known as Hermione) were hosting a dinner party in the ground floor dining room for some of the more well-to-do patrons of the coursing meeting. At eight o'clock the party sat down at table, and no doubt a buzz of genial conversation filled the room as they relaxed in their snug, upholstered surroundings. Sir Frederick, aged 65, was a former Life Guards officer and attaché to the British Embassy in Vienna, and his wife, then in her early fifties, was the eldest daughter of the 12th Duke of Somerset. The couple had married in 1852 and had three sons and five daughters. They would have been most perturbed had they known that their fine home was at that moment under surveillance by some of London's most consummate burglars.

At about 8.15 pm the head housemaid, Margaret Watson, tried to enter Lady Graham's first-floor bedroom but found the door locked from the inside. All had been as usual when a maid had gone up to the room about fifteen minutes earlier. Sir Frederick's valet, Joseph Plenderleath, tried unsuccessfully to break open the door, then ran outside, where he saw a garden seat directly below the open bedroom window, supporting a ladder. Plenderleath climbed up and into the room and realized a break-in had taken place. Lady Graham's dressing-case had been broken open, and lay on the couch. She identified the items missing from it as a pair of long diamond drop earrings, three star-shaped diamond hair ornaments, a ring and a watch-key. A photograph in an oval leather case had also been taken. Their total value was put at about £250, but the room had in fact contained jewellery worth four times as much. The burglar or burglars must have panicked and left the best of the haul behind, including a gold watch lying on the dressing table.

Police officers were soon dispatched to watch the road from Longtown to Carlisle. At about 11 pm 40-year-old Sergeant John Roche was thumping on the door of the police station at Kingstown, a village about seven miles from Longtown and only two miles from Carlisle. When PC Jacob Johnstone appeared at a bedroom window, Roche shouted to him to get dressed as they had to watch the road for burglars. A few minutes later Roche called to Johnstone to come out immediately as he could see some men approaching. Johnstone, a Scotsman in his early thirties, ran out, still in his shirt sleeves and without his coat or helmet. Four figures were

NETHERBY HALL.   THE BURGLARY

The burglars escaping from Netherby Hall. Although four are shown, it was later established that only Rudge, Martin and Baker were at the scene. *Illustrated Police News*

walking towards them in the bright moonlight: Rudge, Martin and Baker, wearing dark overcoats, and a fourth man in a light-coloured coat.

Roche's resonant Irish accent broke the stillness of the night. 'Stop there! Who are you? Where are you coming from, and where are you going to?'

'What business is that of yours?' responded the arrogant Cockney voice of James Baker. 'We're all sporting men.' He tried to push his way past.

'I'm a police officer,' said Roche, 'There's been a serious robbery. You'll have to come to the police station and be searched.'

'I'll give you police officer', snarled Baker, and swung an iron jemmy at Roche's head. The alert officer managed to fend off the weapon with his left hand, and with his right he dealt Baker a hefty blow with his truncheon. Roche was a powerfully built man, described in 1921 by James Walter Brown in *Round Carlisle Cross* as of 'splendid physique, and very powerful . . . He was the biggest – and may I add one of the handsomest – police officers within my recollection.' Baker stumbled under the force of the impact, but Rudge and Martin drew revolvers and fired simultaneously. Roche felt a stab of pain in his arm and was knocked from his feet. The men then fled down the road in the direction of Carlisle, one of them viciously kicking Roche in the head as he attempted to get up.

Despite his injuries, the plucky Roche mustered all his strength and struggled to his feet, determined to assist his comrade who was already in pursuit. Johnstone closed the gap and was attempting to grab the man closest to him when the one at the front turned and fired. Johnstone staggered and fell, a bullet in his chest.

'Oh, sergeant, I'm shot, I'm shot!' he cried.

Roche immediately broke off the chase, and with difficulty managed to get his wounded comrade to his feet. Together they trudged unsteadily back to the police station. Dr Henry Lediard was sent for, and found Johnstone 'very pale and close to death'. Lediard removed a bullet from the right-hand side of Johnstone's chest, and later extracted a bullet close to the main artery of Roche's right arm.

About half a mile away, at the village of Moorville, Sergeant Michael Handley, a Scotsman in his early forties, had heard the sound of two gunshots, which had carried easily across the still night air. He ran to nearby houses for help. Thomas Armstrong, a nurseryman, and George Graham Hetherington, an auctioneer and cattle dealer, bravely ran with Handley in the direction of the gunfire. When they had gone only a few hundred yards they saw four men walking towards them. Handley asked them what the row was about, and was told 'We have been assaulted by two men back there.' The officer gripped the arm of the man in the light-coloured coat and announced he was detaining them. The man, Handley recalled, then 'put a pistol to my breast and said "Oh will you? You bastard!"'

Mr Armstrong lost no time in evaluating their hopeless situation. 'Leave go of him,' he told Handley, 'let's get out of this'. Handley reluctantly released his grip, and the four strangers disappeared into the darkness.

Several hours later, at about 2.30 am, John Strong, gateman of a level-crossing on the Dalston Road in Carlisle, heard footsteps crunching on the gravel outside his cabin. Looking outside he made out the outlines of four men walking along the railway track. A few minutes later PC Christopher Fortune passed on routine patrol, and Strong told him what he had seen. Fortune, an Irishman in his mid-30s, set off briskly after the men along the railway embankment.

The shooting of Roche and Johnstone at Kingstown.
Illustrated Police News

'Hello chaps!' he called out. 'What's to do at this time of the morning?'

They turned to face him, and he was knocked senseless by a vicious blow to the head, probably from an iron jemmy. Fortune regained consciousness some time later to find himself lying at the foot of the embankment. He had indeed been very fortunate. He had been deliberately left lying across the line in the path of the next train. It seems, however, that after going a few yards along the line James Baker had had a twinge of conscience. He returned and rolled the unconscious figure off the railway line and down the embankment. With great difficulty Fortune managed to drag himself two hundred yards along the line to the next signal box. There was so much blood on his face that the signalman, Thomas Evans, thought at first that the wounded man was wearing a mask. Interviewed by the *Carlisle Journal*, he told how he gave Fortune two lidfuls of tea, 'drinking the blood and tea together, poor fellow'. Fortune was found to have nineteen wounds to his skull, three of which were deep incisions. A daylight search revealed his helmet lying near a pool of blood, a piece of his skin stuck to a gash inside it.

The thermometer fell below freezing that Wednesday night as the four fugitives trudged southwards. As dawn began to break they urgently sought a hiding place. According to the *Carlisle Journal*, they 'concealed themselves near Wreay at a place where there is a sort of cave or arrangement of precipitous rocks near the River Petteril'. Another theory held that they took refuge in the woods around Southwaite, approximately six miles south of Carlisle. They were hard men, well used to life's privations, but the circumstances in which they now found themselves must have begun to rattle even their normally steely nerve. It is not difficult to imagine heated dialogue between them as, dog-tired, cold and hungry, they collapsed into sleep. As soon as darkness began to spread its welcome cloak, they roused themselves and started walking south once more,

PC Joseph Byrnes. *Illustrated Police News*

keeping to the line of the railway. At this point Rudge, Martin and Baker are thought to have parted company with the fourth man.

At 7 pm that evening, Thursday 29 October, the trio approached the village of Calthwaite about eleven miles south of Carlisle. Its station-master, John Hayes, had already been told of the events of the previous evening and warned to be on the look-out for the wanted men. He watched as Rudge, Martin and Baker, like three naughty schoolboys, kicked their heels for some time outside the station trying to decide who should make the necessary enquiry. Finally, one of the men ventured in and enquired the time of the next south-bound train. On being told that there were no more that evening, he mumbled something about looking for lodgings and left. Hayes watched them walk away in the direction of Plumpton, a small village some two miles distant.

At 8 pm William Gornall, the station-master at Plumpton, was in his booking-office when a man came to the window and enquired the time of the next train to London. Gornall told the man that there was no train until the next morning, and the stranger thanked him and went back to his two companions who were waiting outside. As soon as they had gone, Gornall lost no time in sending a boy named William Lowthian with a written message to the home of Joseph Byrnes, the local constable. Byrnes was 34 and hailed from the village of Tullyorier near Bambridge in County Down, Ireland. He was a large man, 5 feet $10^1/2$ inches tall and weighing 13 stone. He had been a policeman for eleven years and had become a much-liked and respected pillar of the community which he protected. Byrnes had formerly been a miner, and possessed a natural fellow-feeling with the ordinary working man. He had informed the local railway staff about the Netherby robbery, and the Calthwaite station-master remembered him commenting on the 'folly of one man tackling three armed men'.

When Joseph Byrnes received the news that the armed fugitives had been seen nearby, he immediately got ready to leave. He knew, of course, about the attacks on the police officers Roche, Johnstone and Fortune. In 1876 Byrnes had married Eleanor Bertram, daughter of a police inspector, and the couple now had four children, the youngest just a week old. We are told by the *Carlisle Journal* that 'Mrs Byrnes implored him to be careful; and after a tender leave-taking the brave man assured his wife that he would run no unnecessary risk; but she remarked afterwards "I knew how anxious he was, and I knew he had no fear"'. Byrnes briefly spoke to William Gornall at the railway station, on the outskirts of the village, then left at about 8.10 pm to walk the 3/4 mile or so towards the village centre. Ten minutes later he saw Thomas Simpson, a mason's apprentice, walking towards him and asked whether he had seen three strangers. Simpson replied that yes, three such men had asked the way to the nearest public house. He had directed them towards the Pack Horse, which he himself had just left.

At 8.30 pm the Pack Horse was occupied by perhaps half a dozen local working men relaxing over a pint after a hard day's labour. Ann Griffiths, the landlord's wife, was behind the bar when two men, later identified as Rudge and Baker, entered the pub. They ordered a gill of beer each. Perhaps by now the three were strapped for money; a 'gill' is only a quarter of a pint, and we can imagine that in the present crisis they would have been ready to put away a good deal more liquor than that. The landlady noted that the men appeared to be exhausted. She sent her niece, 13-year-old Margaret Murray, to the cellar to fetch the beer. The men then asked for some bread and cheese to take away, stating that they had been driving all day and had not eaten since early morning. While the food was being prepared they each had another gill of ale and also asked for a pint of rum to be put in a bottle. They said they were in a hurry to catch a train. The men paid 3 shillings and left, having been in the pub for little more than five minutes.

Shortly afterwards, at 8.40 pm, the noise of what sounded like a shot was heard close to the vicarage, 200 yards from the Pack Horse. The vicar was away from home, but his housekeeper, Elizabeth Irving, heard the sound clearly, as did others living nearby. Some time after nine o'clock the lad William Lowthian, who had delivered the message to PC Byrnes, was walking past the vicarage with some

The mortally wounded PC Byrnes is thrown over the wall at Plumpton by Baker (left), Martin (centre) and Rudge (right). *Illustrated Police News*

other villagers when they heard what they thought was a dog growling. At ten o'clock Thomas Lowthian, a slater, left the Pack Horse to make his way home. As he passed a dry stone wall opposite the Vicarage, he heard a strange moaning sound which he at first thought was some animal in distress. Lowthian ran quickly back to the inn to fetch the landlord, William Griffiths, and they returned with a lantern. Behind the wall, which was about 3 ft 6 inches high, they discovered PC Byrnes lying on his back in a pool of blood. He was only barely alive. Lowthian and Mr Griffiths summoned help from the remaining stragglers at the Pack Horse, and Byrnes was laid on a door and carried back to the pub. Medical aid was immediately sent for. William Edward Matthews, assistant to Dr Montgomery, arrived at about midnight, but could do nothing to save Byrnes, who died at 12.50 am. A police officer lay dead; a grieving widow and fatherless children mourned their loss. Events in Cumberland were taking an uncannily similar turn to those enacted in Essex nine months earlier.

The post-mortem later revealed that Joseph Byrnes had been shot in the left eye, the bullet exiting half an inch behind his left ear. His right arm was much discoloured from the wrist to the shoulder, and it seemed that he had been tightly gripped before being shot. Police Sergeant Robert Bremner arrived at about 1.40 am. He was given Byrnes's slouch hat, which displayed two bullet holes. Shown to the place where the body had been found, Bremner saw a pool of blood in the centre of the road, and signs that something had been dragged the ten feet or so from there to the side of the road. The stones on top of the wall were also stained with blood.

Meanwhile, Byrnes's attackers were pressing on southwards. Rudge, according to the *Carlisle Patriot*, was later to say that 'they actually ate the bread and cheese when it was smeared with the blood of their victim, and they did their best to wipe it on their coat cuffs'.

13

'I Suppose I shall be Done for the Romford Murder Now'

At about 10 pm that evening, just as the mortally wounded PC Byrnes was discovered behind the wall at Plumpton, a policeman spotted three men walking in single file along the railway track at Thacka Bridge, about half a mile north of Penrith. This news soon reached the railwaymen at Penrith Station. One of these was 26-year-old Christopher Gaddes, guard of a south-bound goods train which had stopped to detach some wagons. The goods train remained for about fifteen minutes and then, the uncoupling completed, Gaddes gave the signal for the driver to move off. The train began to crawl slowly forward and Gaddes walked back alongside it, preparing to climb up into his guard's van at the rear. Suddenly, from the corner of his eye, he caught sight of three figures darting from the shadows of the goods yard and running towards the train. As the train picked up momentum Gaddes swung himself up into his van. As he did so, he saw the men climb up and drop into one of the wagons.

When his train passed the signal-box south of Penrith station, Gaddes tried to call out to the signalman but was unable to make him hear. Undeterred, Gaddes wrote a note with instructions for a telegraph message to be sent ahead to Tebay informing the station-master that the suspected men were aboard. A short time later, as the train laboured up the steep incline of Shap Summit, Gaddes saw his opportunity and threw his note down onto the foot-plate of a stationary locomotive. The driver picked it up straight away and

THE BRAKESMAN C. GADDES

Christopher Gaddes, the railway guard whose heroics led to the capture of Martin and Rudge. *Illustrated Police News*

quickly read the message. He gave Gaddes the thumbs-up; message understood. Gaddes's train gathered speed and pressed on towards its next stop at Tebay, some eighteen miles further south.

As his train pulled into Tebay Station, at about 11.30 pm, Gaddes saw to his dismay that the message telegraphed from Shap must have been delayed, for it was only just being written out. So no reception party awaited, but the valiant guard lost no time in mustering a squad of equally bold fellow railwaymen and they began a systematic search of the goods wagons. Gaddes then received a shock, as he was to tell the *Carlisle Patriot*: 'When I jumped into the waggon occupied by the burglars, I fell right upon them, and was almost overcome by surprise, as I had mistaken the waggon. We all four quickly scrambled out . . .'

Two men bolted in one direction, the third, who turned out to be Martin, going the opposite way. George Beattie, a foreman porter, was ready; as Martin darted past, Beattie felled him with a well-aimed stroke from a brake-stick three inches in diameter. Martin staggered and slid to the ground, his hand reaching towards his overcoat pocket. By this time, William Parker, an engine- driver, had come up to give Beattie assistance. The two railwaymen quickly overpowered the stunned villain and, on searching his pockets, soon found what he had been frantically trying to grab – a loaded six-chambered revolver. Also in the pocket was a stout length of rope, which was soon put to good use in fastening Martin's hands firmly behind his back.

Rudge, meanwhile, had slipped down beside the bridge which carried the railway across the River Lune. He had been spotted, however, by Robert Willis, another engine-driver, who set off in pursuit. When cornered, Rudge put his right hand into his left breast pocket, and Willis immediately flattened him with a jack-bar. Rudge was soon tied securely to a pillar on the station platform. A search of his coat revealed another gun. The time was now approaching midnight and, although the railwaymen conducted another thorough search of the area, no trace could be found of the third man. The *Carlisle Journal* later reported that:

> The criminals attributed their capture at Tebay to the fact that they had fallen asleep in the train. After entering the goods wagon at Penrith and concealing themselves beneath the tarpaulin sheet, they were so weary that they fell asleep on the journey to Tebay, and never wakened up until Gaddes jumped upon the tarpaulin at Tebay. Then the three hunted men jumped up, dazed and ignorant of their whereabouts. . . . Rudge often muttered 'curses, not loud but deep', about that sleep beneath the tarpaulin. He had no spare cartridges; but Martin had . . . He knew they were in for murder already, and their only desperate aim now was to escape at all hazards.

Rudge tied to a pillar at Tebay Station after being captured by the railwaymen. *Illustrated Police News*

THE CAPTURE

The same newspaper also quoted Rudge as saying that 'if he had been able to get at his revolver fast enough he would have made every loaded chamber tell its tale upon the railway men at Tebay':

> Pursuing the policy which they had adopted all through their visit into Cumberland of changing caps and coats, in order to render positive identification difficult, there is no doubt that Rudge and Martin had changed coats between Plumpton and Tebay, and Rudge, accustomed to carry his revolver in his left breast pocket, put his right hand in his left breast to pull out his weapon when the railway men were closing upon him; but the breast pocket in the coat he had on at the time was on the right hand side, and before he could remedy his mistake the irresistible jack-bar was on his head.

It was not long before the third fugitive, James Baker, was sighted again. At midnight Thomas Matley, the driver of a goods train leaving Tebay, noticed a man about 250 yards from the south platform end. Matley remembered that 'He sprang for the fourth wagon after the engine had passed him. I was sure he had either got in the train or had fallen under it. When I arrived at Oxenholme I sent my fireman to telephone to see if there were any police about. Two policemen and a sergeant came and searched the train but found no one.' As the goods train made its way towards Lancaster, a journey of over two hours, Baker must have got off at every stop while the train was searched and then leapt on board again when it moved off. The *Carlisle Journal* later wrote admiringly that 'The journey of Baker from

Tebay to Lancaster is one of the most extraordinary incidents of the case. In leaping upon the moving wagons, which have no foothold except the axle boxes, he displayed the skill and courage of a trapezist. A slip would have meant death.'

At 2.20 am a passenger train en route from Carlisle to London stopped at Lancaster Station. Henry Cooper, the guard, was standing on the platform when a man stepped out of the darkness and asked 'Is this the train for Crewe way?' Cooper, of course, had heard all about the burglary at Netherby and the ensuing manhunt – in fact Superintendent Russell had just travelled alongside him in the guard's van from Carlisle to Tebay on his way to collect Rudge and Martin. Cooper studied the man warily.

'Crewe way?' he snapped. 'Where do you want to go?'

'Oh, Liverpool, or, well, anywhere really,' the man replied, vaguely.

'Have you got your ticket?'

'No. Where can I get one?'

'Where have you come from?'

'Down the yard past the policeman. I've spoken to the policeman.'

'That's funny, at this time of the morning.'

The man said he'd been 'galling it', or enjoying private time with a girlfriend. Cooper had noticed that his face was covered with spots of soot. 'You're the fellow that's wanted by the police!' he said, and grabbed him by the shoulder. The stranger turned and tried to get away, but Cooper seized him and forced his overcoat down his back, effectively pinioning his arms. Cooper's call for help brought two more railway employees running to the scene and James Baker was at last overpowered and secured to await the arrival of the authorities. It was noted that his coat, like those of Rudge and Martin, was smeared with blood down the front.

The next morning, during a search of the riverside spot where Rudge had been captured, a key and an earring were discovered in the water. Their finder, local man John Wilson, stated that 'From where I found the key lying it must have been thrown by somebody under the bridge – it could not have been thrown from a train.'

Anthony Rudge and John Martin were taken to Carlisle's Earl Street Police Station in the early hours of Friday 30 October. By the time the train carrying James Baker pulled in at about 1 pm that day, the murder of PC Byrnes had become public knowledge, and feelings were running high. The press reported that

A crowd of thousands of people burst into the station by every inlet and took possession of the platform. As soon as the train arrived they swarmed upon the carriages, and crowded around the prisoner, striking at him with sticks, hooting and excoriating him in an almost indescribable manner . . . had it not been for the exertions of the Chief Constable the prisoner would have been lynched by the infuriated people who were surging around.

One man did succeed in grabbing Baker's hair, but eventually the police were able to get him into the comparative safety of the station refreshment room and lock the door. There they had to endure a tense period of uncertainty until the captive could be transferred to join his companions at the Earl Street lock-up.

Interviewed separately by Superintendent John Douglas Sempill, the trio retained sufficient presence of mind to establish — superficially, at least — a feasible line of defence. Rudge gave his occupation as dog-trainer, and maintained that he had attended the coursing meeting at Longtown in a purely professional capacity. He claimed to be 45, but observers noted that he appeared younger, as of course he was. Rudge was described as 'of middle-sized stature, with a clean shaven, round face and a black moustache. He is broad-shouldered, and has the bearing of a man who has undergone military training.'

John Martin was 'a man of taller and more slender build . . . He has rather a long face with scrubby brown moustache and short, close cut whiskers. He was dressed in a greasy suit of dark tweed and wore a greasy-looking black silk peaked cap . . . He had upon his head a severe bruise, the effect of a blow with a stick, and this may possibly have been received when the railwaymen were securing him at Tebay.' Martin described himself as a bookie's runner who, like Rudge, had been at the meeting solely in pursuance of his livelihood. He claimed he had met Rudge in a pub only a short time before they had boarded the goods train, both having missed the last train of the evening for London. Both explained they had revolvers for self-defence when carrying large amounts of cash in connection with their gambling activities.

Baker, on the other hand, told the truth when asked his identity. He stated that he lived at 106 Montague Street, Bethnal Green, where he carried on a business as a greengrocer and general dealer in provisions. He claimed he had attended the coursing meeting on Tuesday and Wednesday, but had left on Wednesday evening for Newcastle where he had spent the night at a brothel. He had returned to Carlisle, he said, on Thursday evening and had travelled to Lancaster by passenger train. A journalist noted that 'His figure is known to many Carlisle people, as a frequenter of the Carlisle racecourse'.

Superintendent Sempill already possessed important evidence in the form of the three portmanteaus which the men had left at Gretna Station. Apart from changes of clothes, the bags contained skeleton keys, a safe-breaking chisel, which could be used as a jemmy by putting a handle into it, a lantern, a piece of new, strong rope

Martin (seated) speaking to Rudge about the Simmons murder in their cell.
Illustrated Police News

and a pouch of revolver cartridges. When Rudge had been searched, one pocket was found to contain a broken bottle of rum. Some of the liquid remained in the bottle, but most had seeped out, saturating the pocket. This provided direct evidence linking Rudge with the purchase of the bottle of rum in the Pack Horse at Plumpton. Sempill took the men's statements and then formally charged all three with the robbery at Netherby, with firing at Roche and Johnstone with intent to murder, and with the murder of Constable Byrnes. Rudge and Martin made no reply, while Baker merely repeated that, at the time of the alleged offences, he had been in Newcastle.

From what we know of the characters of Rudge and Martin it is safe to assume that they would defiantly tough it out to the end. Like Adams before them, they viewed the ultimate penalty of the law as preferable to the ordeal of years of penal servitude. James Baker, however, only 28, and with a legitimate business and a woman waiting for him in London, may not have viewed the prospect of a premature and ignominious death with such complacency. He lay in his cold cell at Earl Street Police Station, ghostly pale and aching from head to toe from his exertions. He had asked for a telegram to be sent to Nellie explaining that he was 'in trouble', and she soon caught a train from London to Carlisle in order to be with him. Baker declared to Nellie that 'he would never allow them to hang him', and promptly went on hunger strike. After three days a doctor persuaded him to take food again, but he remained in a depressed state of mind.

On Friday 30 October, the inquest on Joseph Byrnes opened at the Pack Horse before John Carrick, coroner for the eastern division of Cumberland. Only one witness, Sergeant Robert Bremner, was called. After he had formally identified the body, the inquest was adjourned. On Saturday 31 October the trio, handcuffed and wearing leg-irons, were brought before the county magistrates and remanded in custody for a week. When the inquest resumed on Friday 6 November, the jury heard from several witnesses before giving a verdict of wilful murder against Rudge, Martin and Baker.

Within hours of the apprehension of the fugitives, the London police had been contacted in the hope that they could identify them. In response, a train arriving in Carlisle on the morning of Sunday 1 November 1885 carried among its passengers Chief Inspector John Shore and Detective Sergeant William Elias Rolfe. They were able to provide the Cumberland authorities with an abundance of information about the past escapades of the roguish trio. It is not difficult to imagine Rolfe's satisfaction as he peered through the observation hole in the door of John Martin's cell. Martin was 'identified as the man who shot the gardener at Lord Sheffield's place, near Bournemouth, on the occasion of an attempted burglary 12 months ago'. Yet this startling claim was overshadowed by the announcement that Martin was a suspect in the Simmons case, 'one of the most daring and dastardly murders of modern times'. Rudge and Martin had been housed together, and no doubt a guard had his ear to their door at all times. The *Carlisle Patriot* reported that Martin 'has made several allusions to the crime. He has remarked to Rudge, who is in the same cell with him, "I suppose I shall be done for the Romford murder now"'.

Later on the day of their arrival in Carlisle, Sunday 1 November 1885, detectives Rolfe and Shore may have attended the funeral of Joseph Byrnes at Penrith Cemetery. A huge crowd of some 2,000 people were present to pay their respects. Mrs Eleanor Byrnes had received visits of condolence from, among others, Lady Graham and one of her daughters. Queen Victoria herself sent a letter to the Cumberland police expressing her sorrow at the murder and enquiring after the wounded officers. It was announced that the eldest Byrnes child, $9^{1}/_{2}$-year-old Edward, would be given a place at the Metropolitan and City Police Orphanage at Twickenham in Middlesex, to be followed in due course by his younger brother when he reached the age of 7.

Two days later, on Tuesday 3 November, an identity parade was held at Earl Street Police Station. In preparation, Rudge, Martin and Baker were visited by a barber. Martin, we are told, 'jocularly asked whether they were to be honoured with a visit from the Mayor'. The witnesses summoned to attend, including the

The grave of PC Byrnes in Penrith Cemetery, marked by a stone erected in 2006.
Brian Norman

station-masters from Gretna and Calthwaite and Mrs Ann Griffiths and her niece Margaret Murray from the Pack Horse, were shown a line-up of between six and eight men with a sheet placed across their ankles and feet to conceal the leg-irons which the arrested trio still wore.

Several witnesses picked out Rudge, Martin and Baker, but there must have been a fleeting moment of amusement when Thomas Lowthian, who had discovered the body of Byrnes, tapped on the shoulder of a man whom he thought he had seen near Plumpton Station on the evening of the murder. He had picked out Detective Sergeant William Rolfe! Before returning to London later that day, Rolfe interviewed Baker, who remarked that he would probably never see him again. Yet Baker could have derived some solace from the knowledge that his father, who was preparing to make the journey to Carlisle, had arranged for him to be represented by a solicitor, Mr W Moore of Bow. Mr Moore would subsequently engage a barrister to plead Baker's case at the trial.

Rudge, Martin and Baker were brought up again before the Carlisle magistrates. An early witness was an elderly lady named Mary Richardson, who stated that while at work 'breaking thorns or hedge slashing' on the Netherby Hall estate, at about 11.40 am on Wednesday 28 October, she was approached by three men wearing long dark coats. One, later identified as Rudge, asked her if the master of 'the big house' was at home. A carter named William Atkinson then told the magistrates that at about 12.45 pm he too had met the trio on the Netherby to Longtown road and was asked the same question. Rudge had casually remarked that he thought he would have seen Sir Frederick at the coursing.

Monday 23 November saw the final day of the magistrates' court hearings. The public clamoured to be admitted. According to the *Carlisle Journal*, 'Ladies flocked to the Court every day, and one of these was so much interested in the prisoners that she was most anxious to provide them with wine for their dinner when they were before the magistrates.' Predictably, the Chief Constable refused her request. Local press reports kept the public up to date with every relevant tit-bit of information concerning the defendants, their general appearance and their demeanour in court. The journalists had soon picked up on Anthony Rudge's swaggering self-assertiveness. From the outset Rudge made copious notes of the evidence. He also exploited every opportunity to employ his right of cross-examination to browbeat witnesses and attempt to impugn their credibility.

One such deponent who was to fall foul of Rudge's ire was David Johnstone, of the Graham Arms in Gretna, who described how he had seen bunches of keys and other incriminating articles removed from the portmanteau before the men left for the railway station.

'You say that three of us went up to the station?' Rudge quizzed the witness. 'Was this directly after locking the bag up?'

Johnstone was momentarily taken aback at being addressed from the dock. Turning to the magistrate, he asked incredulously, 'Am I to answer the prisoner's question, sir?' Mr Horrocks, the chief magistrate, informed him that he must.

'Yes, of course you must,' Rudge chaffed. 'And there is another question I would

Rudge, Martin and Baker appearing before the magistrates. *Illustrated Police News*

like to ask you. Do you know the nature of an oath? Do you know when you kiss the book the penalties that attach to telling a lie? Where you go to?'

'Yes' replied Johnstone.

'Where?'

Johnstone considered for a moment, then retorted with an answer which must have pierced the egotistical 'Attorney-General' like a dagger: 'Just where I expect you are going, sir.'

'You may keep you personal remarks to yourself!' Rudge exploded, as laughter burst forth in the courtroom.

Throughout the hearing Rudge remained the most vociferous of the three defendants, bolstered by an occasional intervention by Baker. Much of their cross-examination consisted of attempts to discredit the evidence of identification by stressing details of coats and hats. Martin, on the other hand, seemed already to have accepted his fate. 'What's the use of asking any questions?' was his morose reply when asked if he wished to put anything to the witness.

Though still showing signs of obvious strain, Baker had maintained enough of his spirit to attempt his own exchange with David Johnstone. His brief display of Cockney wit was to introduce another fleeting ripple of amusement into the grim proceedings.

'What did you first say after you first saw the three men?' Baker asked.

Johnstone was clearly determined to be obstructive. 'Speak a little louder please; I'm a little hard of hearing in this ear.'

'Then turn round the other then, and you will be able to catch it fast enough!' cried Baker.

'I told you to step into that room. I only identified two of you. After I saw you I went into the kitchen and said there were thieves in the house, and that they had better take care.'

'How did you know there were thieves in the house?'

'By your looks.'

'Did you not think we looked as well as you?' Baker demanded.

'No, I did not!'

'If I were going to take a thief,' interposed Rudge, '*you* are the first man I would take.'

The magistrates announced that the three would stand trial at the Assizes the following January. They were transferred from the police station cells to Carlisle Gaol. On 29 November it was James Baker's twenty-ninth birthday. His state of mind was, as we have seen, giving the authorities cause for concern. Joseph Leavers, the governor of the gaol, decided to place him in a cell with two other men, John Watson and Robert Cummings, who had been locked up for the relatively trivial offence of failing to provide sureties relating to breach of the peace.

The police, of course, continued to sift every scrap of evidence. The weapons found on Rudge and Martin were examined closely. Rudge's revolver was a powerful, expensive five-chambered 'Bulldog', manufactured in Birmingham. Martin's was a cheaper, Continental, six-chambered revolver of smaller calibre, firing a bullet by fulminate of mercury instead of gunpowder. The bullet extracted from PC Johnstone fitted the gun found on Rudge. The one that had wounded Sergeant Roche fitted Martin's revolver, as did a bullet found on the road nearby.

On 12 December PC Thomas Scott, who had spent eight days diving in the icy waters of the River Lune near the spot where Rudge had made his last defiant stand, finally discovered a gutta-percha rubber tobacco pouch containing a diamond earring and the other small items of jewellery taken from Lady Graham's bedroom. This discovery added yet more weight to the police's case against the three men.

14

'Equally Guilty and Each Deserving Death'

At 10.20 am on Monday 18 January 1886 the trial of Rudge, Martin and Baker got under way at the Carlisle Assizes. It was seen as the most significant trial in Cumberland since Bonnie Prince Charlie's Jacobite rebels were tried and condemned at Carlisle a hundred and forty years earlier. The judge on this occasion was Mr Justice Day, whose full name was Sir John Charles Frederick Sigismund Day. He was then in his sixtieth year, having been born at The Hague in 1826, the son of an army officer. Having chosen to enter the law, he had gained a degree from London University and studied at the Middle Temple before being called to the Bar in January 1849. He became a QC in 1872, and ten years later was made a judge of the Queen's Bench Division at the High Court and awarded a knighthood. Although considered in his private life to be a kind-hearted man, Mr Justice Day, who died in 1908, had a fearsome reputation when acting in the capacity of dispenser of the law. He was a great enthusiast for the effectiveness of the 'cat', and even where relatively minor offences had been committed his sentences were remarkably severe.

The *Carlisle Patriot* reported that the three defendants were looking a little smarter than on their last public appearance, with hair and whiskers neatly trimmed. It also noted, however, that Baker was looking increasingly ashen and ill, 'his lips and fingers twitching all through'. Rudge was his usual alert self, but Martin 'seemed sluggish, and indifferently observant. A greater contrast than that between his apathy and the determined and keen vigilance of his associate could not be well imagined.' The three pleaded not guilty to all charges.

Proceedings began with the case for the prosecution, headed by 50-year-old Ralph Daniel Makinson Littler. He had been a barrister for nearly thirty years, twelve of them as a QC. In later life he would earn a formidable reputation as the 'Terror of the Middlesex Sessions', of which he was chairman for nineteen years, being notorious for the savagery of his sentences. Mr Littler was also a high-ranking Freemason and Chairman of Middlesex County Council from 1889. He was knighted in 1902 and died in 1908. Mr Littler was assisted on this occasion by Henry G Shee (the second son of Mr Justice Shee of the Queen's Bench), and Henry Fell. An early witness called by the prosecution was Rudge's arch-enemy from the magistrates' hearing, David Johnstone. The staid atmosphere of the Assize court and the saturnine glare of the judge prevented a repetition of the shenanigans of the earlier appearance. Lady Hermione Graham was also called, and identified the jewellery found by the police diver in the River Lune.

The three injured police officers also gave their accounts of events. John Roche, now promoted to inspector, was first to take the stand. He was followed by Jacob Johnstone, who appeared very weak and was allowed to sit while giving his evidence. Christopher Fortune was then called. He was still very frail from his recent ordeal and, like Johnstone, was allowed to remain seated. The *Carlisle Patriot* noted that 'The spectators who knew what hale, robust men Johnstone and Fortune were formerly, were much shocked at the evident suffering they had undergone.' Fortune would never recover fully from the brutal attack. He identified the three men in the dock, and the judge overruled an objection from the defence that he had not previously seen them 'mixed with other men'.

Throughout the day's proceedings so far the three defendants had remained sullen and subdued. Now, however, Rudge's frustration got the better of him. 'Well, all I can say is this is like murdering men!' he cried.

James Baker's defence counsel was Miles Walker Mattinson (later Sir Miles), who had been born in Newcastle in 1854 and called to the Bar at Gray's Inn in 1877. He later served as MP for Walton, Liverpool, from 1888 to 1892, and was eventually appointed King's Counsel and Master of Gray's Inn. He was assisted by junior barrister James Lumb. Rudge and Martin were jointly represented by Christopher Cavanagh, a Dubliner in his mid-thirties who had been called to the Bar at the Middle Temple in 1874. Mr Cavanagh had unsuccessfully applied to have the trial held elsewhere because of the depth of feeling in the Carlisle area. His case for the defence of Rudge and Martin appeared to hinge primarily on the matter of identity. The *Carlisle Patriot* noted that 'A very short time sufficed to show that Mr Cavanagh was bent upon fighting every point, and especially that he was bent upon impeaching the honesty of the police.'

The trial resumed at 10 am the next day, Tuesday 19 January. The morning dawned cold and frosty and there was a covering of snow on the ground, but that did not deter the holders of tickets for the public gallery. The questioning now turned to the circumstances of the murder of PC Byrnes. Much of the interrogation concentrated on pinpointing the exact time at which the shooting had occurred. To no one's great surprise, it was discovered that the various clocks in the Pack Horse, Plumpton Railway Station and in homes in the village did not display the same time.

The prisoners now showed little trace of the spirited audacity they had displayed earlier. Just now and then a whispered comment passed between them. Each slab of evidence, delivered by witnesses unwavering in their recall of events, dropped firmly into place like the slamming of a great door. Rudge, ever the 'Attorney-General', still scribbled notes continuously. Perhaps he believed he might still, even at this eleventh hour, find a loophole somewhere in the evidence. Throughout, Rudge flaunted an air of cocksure disparagement of the proceedings. He no doubt thought he was impressing his audience with his knowledge of the law and his composure in the face of adversity, but in fact he gave the impression of being intelligent but chillingly callous.

The evidence then turned to the capture of the fugitives. A ripple of excitement went through the crowded courtroom at the appearance in the witness box of Christopher Gaddes, the goods train guard, regarded as the hero of the hour. Gaddes was 5 feet 9 inches tall with brown hair and blue eyes. He had been born at Longtown, and by a strange coincidence had formerly worked as the driver of the Netherby Estate game cart. At the end of the previous month, December 1885, he had married Catherine Hodgson in Longtown Parish Church. It is easy to imagine the crowds of sightseers waiting for the couple to emerge after the ceremony.

Later that day Superintendent Russell entered the witness box, and described how he took the three into custody and searched them. Mr Cavanagh handed him a key.

'Is that the key you claim to have found in Baker's possession?'

'I cannot swear to it. The ticket is not on it now.'

It was then revealed that this key had been substituted for the real one. Amidst a burst of laughter in the court the incriminating key was then miraculously produced, still bearing its identification label.

'I'm too old a bird to be caught out like that, Sir', quipped Russell.

The third and final day of the trial was Wednesday 20 January 1886. The *Carlisle Patriot* reported that 'Rudge took his place somewhat jauntily, smiling. He nodded to his brother, who is very like him, and who, sitting on the bench for waiting jurymen behind the dock, passed notes to him throughout the day. Martin's apparent unconcern was maintained to the last; there was no less curious spectator in Court. Baker, whose aged father stood in the lobby near, ineffectually laboured to control the manifestation of his anxiety.'

BAKER.   MARTIN.   RUDGE.

Drawings of Rudge, Martin and Baker in court. *Carlisle Journal*

Several witnesses came forward to describe the capture of James Baker at Lancaster. Later, to general surprise, the prosecution called John Watson, an elderly man who, as we have seen, had shared a cell with Baker at Carlisle Gaol. The defence barristers protested, but the judge ruled that Watson should be allowed to speak. His evidence was devastating. Baker, he said, had given a detailed account of the killing of Joseph Byrnes. Baker had confessed that

> the officer asked them who and what they were, and walked towards Baker to arrest him, saying he would have one of them. A struggle now took place which doubtless caused the bruises upon Byrnes's wrist. Baker flourished the stick which he had cut during the day, and struck Byrnes a blow above the eye . . . Martin came up behind Baker, who was in front of Byrnes, and fired the fatal shot.

Later, fleeting moments of amusement occurred when Mr Cavanagh was cross-examining Superintendent Sempill about the arrangements for the identity parade. He suggested it had been rigged because the suspects were still wearing leg-irons and would thus have stood out from the others in the line-up. Sempill protested that 'these did not incommode them in the slightest degree. It would not make them appear stiff – the irons would be no more than three or four pounds in weight.' At this, Rudge's mocking laughter rang out across the stillness of the court. 'The chains are twenty pounds!' he shrieked. 'Eighteen or twenty pounds!'

Eventually, it was time for Mr Littler to make his final speech for the prosecution. He spoke for an hour. Who, he asked, would have had a motive for such a terrible crime as the murder of Byrnes? The answer had to be the people who had committed the robbery at Netherby Hall and the assaults on the police officers at Kingstown and Carlisle. If it were accepted that the three defendants were, indeed, the persons who had carried out these attacks on Roche, Johnstone and Fortune, then it was fair to assume they would be prepared to commit further violence, even murder, to enable their escape. They must have shot PC Byrnes as soon as he challenged them, before he could raise the alarm. The timing of the sound of the shot was proved to coincide to within a minute or so with the time Rudge and Baker left the Pack Horse.

Defence barristers Mr Cavanagh and Mr Mattinson did not call witnesses, but each addressed the jury. Cavanagh suggested that not two but all three men had been in the Pack Horse at the time of the murder. The inn, he said, had various recesses where a man might sit without the landlady being aware he was there. The actual shooting, Mr Cavanagh submitted, was carried out by the mysterious Fourth Man who had then left the group in order to dispose of his incriminating light-coloured coat.

In defence of Baker, Mr Mattinson stated that the evidence indicated that PC Byrnes had been shot by one man acting alone, and that at the time of the shot Baker had been in the Pack Horse with Rudge. He warned the jury that

> If I have failed in my duty today, or if you err in the discharge of your duty, neither my neglect nor your error can ever be repaired in this world. Any one of these men convicted of this terrible crime will pass today from the sight of living men – there is no hand of mercy stretched forth to avert the doom which His Lordship must pass upon him.

Summing up, Mr Justice Day said that if the jury found that all three had manhandled the body over the wall after the shooting – and their bloodstained coats indicated that they had – then all were complicit in the act and were, therefore, all guilty of wilful murder. As we have seen, Byrnes weighed around 13 stone, and the prosecution had maintained that it would have been almost impossible for one person alone to have dragged his body to the 3 feet 6 inch wall and then thrown it over.

The jury retired to their room at 7.15 pm. Rudge, Martin and Baker were allowed to stand down to the rear of the dock, where they chatted with the governor. Baker's father Thomas, only in his fifties but appearing to observers as an elderly and broken man, stood behind the dock, his head resting against the partition and his eyes closed. Rudge's younger brother Thomas Fennell was also present. He seemed more anxious than Rudge himself. When the jury returned at 8.20 pm, the prisoners were called to the front. The *Carlisle Patriot* noted that 'they stepped forward with alacrity, and never looked in the direction of the jury until they had taken their seats, when they simultaneously bent a somewhat nonchalant gaze upon the arbiters of their doom'.

The jury foreman returned guilty verdicts on all three. On being asked whether he had anything to say as to why sentence of death should not now be passed, Rudge, characteristically, spent ten minutes denouncing the evidence. The experts, he said, had measured the wound in Byrnes's skull as 3/8 of an inch in diameter, so it could not have been caused by a bullet from his pistol, which had a half-inch bore. In his turn, Martin answered: 'What is the use of saying anything. It's all settled.' The *Carlisle Journal* noted that 'the brutal expression in his face showed how fierce was the nature that was hidden behind the stolid countenance'. Baker, in a weak voice, said: 'The prosecution gave evidence that the fatal shot was fired at a certain time, and it is proved by the prosecution that I was in the public house at the time the fatal shot was fired.'

Striking his hand on the ledge before him, Rudge interrupted, demanding why the skull of Joseph Byrnes had not been produced. 'That would have settled the point', he declared. 'But what is the good of saying anything now? Our former crimes would naturally tend to make the jury think such men as us should be got rid of.' He paused, then made a dramatic announcement.

'I confess to the murder myself! I own it! Although I say I own it, you cannot prove it. No one else was there but myself – not a soul, and yet the bullet that came from my pistol did not do it!'

Amidst murmurs of horror from the galleries, Rudge claimed that

> In passing death upon me, you are passing the sentence on me that I want – that I absolutely want. I prefer it to going into the living death of penal servitude. I know what that is; I have been through it, where a man is thrust into himself, and the iron, as it were, is forced into his soul, and has no outcome . . . If you hang these two men, you are committing judicial murder!

Eventually Rudge came to a halt, and the attention of the hushed court now turned to Mr Justice Day, his already cadaverous features ghastly in the glare of the gaslight and rendered even more sinister by the black cap placed upon his wig. He told the three men that 'the evidence on which you stand convicted is overwhelming', and pronounced the dread sentence of hanging. The prisoners were taken away. The *Carlisle Patriot* told its readers that 'Rudge was the last to go down the prison stairs, and, laughing, he made some remark to Baker who was in front of him.' It was 8.45 pm when the court finally fell silent, exactly a year to the day since Inspector Thomas Simmons had been shot and mortally wounded.

Newspapers were united in their approval of the verdict. According to the *Daily Telegraph*, 'No criminals will go more justly to their doom than Rudge, Baker and Martin, caught red-handed in robbery and savage warfare against their kind – all equally guilty and each deserving death.' The *Scotsman* commented that 'This trial closes one of the most remarkable stories of crime that have recently come before the courts. The prisoners were of the type of burglar and desperado that is met with more frequently in the "Penny Dreadfuls" than in the dock.'

15
'Goodbye, Old Pal!'

Back at Carlisle Gaol, the condemned men now experienced a relaxation of the usually strict dietary regime. According to the *Carlisle Patriot*, 'They had the option of tea or cocoa morning and afternoon, instead of the usual porridge; and instead of the alternate soup or pudding for dinner, they had fish or mutton chop. Rudge and Martin were allowed to smoke, which was a great comfort. Baker did not seek this indulgence. Rudge also asked for beer, but this the authorities could not allow.'

Rudge now spent a great deal of time on a lengthy manuscript on the subject of the convict system. Harking back to the theme of his speech at the trial, he wrote that of all the terrors awaiting the convict, including the 'cat' and hard labour, it was the long periods of silent, solitary confinement which had filled him with the greatest dread and had contributed most to his alienation from honest society. He asserted that the three major causes of crime were heredity, locality and the police system. Rudge intended his manuscript to be sent to the Howard League (now the Howard League for Penal Reform), but it was instead

NEWGATE—THE CONDEMNED CELL

A condemned cell, showing the prisoner being watched at all times. *From W J Loftie, London City (1891)*

forwarded to the Home Office, where, according to a cynical *Carlisle Journal* reporter, 'no doubt it will be pigeon-holed'.

It was announced that the executions would take place on Monday 8 February. Within their separate cells, the men were never left alone, and alleged snippets of conversation with visitors and prison staff were passed on to an eager public via the newspaper columns. The *Carlisle Journal* claimed, for example, that Rudge declared that the Netherby affair was not a planned burglary, and he now looked back at it 'with contempt'. Apparently, 'It was carried out to Baker's plans, and we hear that Rudge has since expressed his regret that his own scheme of operations had not been carried out, as he believes that would have been more successful, and they might have got clear away.' Rudge, it seems, normally carried a large-scale Ordnance Survey map of the area in order to make a quick getaway using lesser-known routes. The Netherby robbery, apparently, 'was only taken up on the spur of the moment, upon a hint received when the three were attending Longtown coursing "to pick up a bit of money"'.

Rudge seemed genuinely indifferent to his impending fate. His brother remarked that the sound of the men working on the construction of the scaffold near his cell must be distressing. 'Oh, you need not trouble about that', replied Rudge. 'It would not affect me if they were putting it up at my bed-head.'

Stories circulated linking Rudge with James Berry, who would again be called upon to act as hangman. One rumour stated that Rudge had met Berry some years previously at Doncaster racecourse, and offered a bet of £13 to £2 that he would never hang him. Another was that the pair had met on a train journey, and in the course of conversation Berry had mentioned he was the public hangman. On leaving the train Rudge had turned to Berry and said 'Well, I hope I never meet you in a professional capacity.'

John Martin, it seems, was much less communicative. According to the *Carlisle Journal*:

> He is the plodding burglar, doing best when working to his own hand, and he now expressed regret that at that meeting in London . . . he consented to join the gang. He says that now his fate is sealed it is of no use whining about it. He has lost the game and must stand by the result . . . He is not a man to 'peach', and when, before the trial, Rudge was disposed to tell his solicitor the history of the whole transaction, Martin interposed with a protest against 'letting 'em know any more about it'.

The *Carlisle Patriot* stated that 'Though, as yet, Martin's previous career is but imperfectly known, it seems that he is a criminal of note. If, he says, he had only dropped one word to Rolfe, that officer would have been able, at once, to associate him with a whole series of startling robberies which have perplexed the London police.'

It seems that William Rolfe was unable to persuade Martin to admit to any involvement in the Simmons case. The *Carlisle Journal* claimed, however, that Martin had confessed to being at the scene when Inspector Simmons was shot, but that Adams had been the actual gunman. It was reported that Martin's relatives did not visit him in prison, although they did write to the authorities asking about his welfare.

James Baker remained nervous and depressed. He clung to the fragile prospect of a reprieve, knowing that his family had been campaigning desperately on his behalf on the grounds that he did not fire the fatal shot, and that he was under the domination of the others. According to the *Carlisle Journal*, 'some of the family we believe even journeyed to Osborne to try and see the Queen and intercede with Her Majesty for his life. In that mission, however, they were not successful.' Baker received visits from his father, mother, brother, two sisters and brother-in-law. His sweetheart Nellie, the first person to be summoned to Carlisle after Baker's arrest, also made the journey from London more than once.

Baker was the subject of a strange coincidence connected to PC Jacob Johnstone, who had been shot along with Sergeant John Roche at Kingstown. A few days before the shooting Johnstone, investigating some local thefts, had been sent five or six photographs of criminals discharged from Pentonville Prison. On recovering from his wounds, Johnstone began to look through the photographs. According to the *Carlisle Patriot*, 'he paused suddenly at one, and exclaimed "That little fellow was one of the chaps that shot at Roche and me!" It was Baker's photograph.'

On Friday 5 February, three days before the date fixed for their execution, the men said farewell to their final visitors. It was reported in the *Carlisle Journal* that for Baker's parents, brothers and sisters, 'It was no time for reproaches, though full of regrets. Baker had always been a trouble to his friends, a thief and a housebreaker by profession, and now the end had come at last.' Rudge had told his brother Thomas that he particularly wanted to see once more his 3-year-old nephew, who had been named after him, and this wish was granted.

On Sunday evening Baker sat down to write his last letter, addressed to Nellie. In the early hours of the morning Rudge and Martin were visited by Canon Waterton, a Catholic priest who had attended them throughout their imprisonment. Martin asked him to make it publicly known that he, not Rudge, had fired the shot that killed Joseph Byrnes. He claimed that he had not intended to murder the constable, but to disable him so that they could get away.

The morning of Monday 8 February 1886 dawned cold, dark and dismal. James Berry would be celebrating his thirty-fourth birthday by carrying out his very first triple execution. Berry had been handing out a business card during his stay in Carlisle, described in the *Carlisle Patriot* as 'a pretty little production, – a pale green ground; the device, a sprig of maidenhair fern, printed in gold, like the border; in one corner, the words, "James Berry, executioner", and in the other corner, "I, Bilton Place, Bradford, Yorks"'. Berry's reputation had taken a knock barely more than two months previously, on 30 November 1885, when he had miscalculated the length of drop at the execution of Robert Goodale at Norwich Castle. The condemned man had been about 6 feet tall and 16 stone in weight, and to the horror of onlookers he was completely decapitated.

Berry tested the Carlisle gallows and expressed his confidence that it would work 'as nice as ninepence'. He had brought with him an assistant calling himself Charles Maldon. This was, in fact, the pseudonym of 38-year-old Sir Claude Champion de Crespigny, 4th baronet, of Champion Lodge, Great Totham in Essex. Sir Claude was a renowned military adventurer with great prowess in many sports such as steeplechase riding, swimming and ballooning. Sir Claude had, as we have seen, insisted on being present at the execution of Adams at Chelmsford the previous year. He now wished to be a more active participant in this final, terrible act of the law. The *Essex Standard* noted drily that 'Probably the unfortunate culprits were quite unaware of the unprecedented honour that was being done to them.' Questions were later asked in the House of Commons about Sir Claude's behaviour, and *Punch* magazine suggested he had better alter his name to 'Sir Claude de Crespiniony'.

At 6.30 am Rudge, Martin and Baker were brought cups of tea by the governor's wife, Emma Leavers. At about 7.45 the prison bell began to sound its dreadful toll, and ten minutes later Berry and his assistant entered the cells with the pinioning straps. De Crespigny recalled that 'Berry went into Martin's cell, and I went into Baker's, and pinioned his arms. Then Berry pinioned Rudge. . . . All three men bore themselves well, and gave no trouble. Martin was calm and collected; indeed, as I understand, he had from the first showed himself to be a man of great fortitude and determination.'

Just before 8 am Baker and Martin were brought out of their cells, their collars and neckties off and their hair dishevelled. The *Carlisle Patriot* reported that Baker

> had a dazed expression in his eyes, as if he were looking beyond the scene before him, and he seemed to sway or stagger as, supported by the Chaplain and the warders, he walked across the hall to the west door. Martin was perfectly

collected. At the door, a pause of half a minute was made, before Rudge was brought out. The latter looked with eager gaze among the throng, and, pushing his way, rather than being led, to where Martin and Baker stood, he shook hands with each, and the valediction 'Goodbye old pal!' passed between them in undertones.

The three were meeting for the first time since their trial. The warders also shook hands with the condemned men, bidding them 'Goodbye' and 'God bless you!'

Baker, accompanied by the prison chaplain, headed the procession the short distance across the prison yard to a gallows facing the blank brick wall inside the old treadmill shed, beneath which a pit 10 feet deep had been dug. Their names had been written in chalk where each was to stand – Martin in the centre, with Rudge on his right and Baker on his left. Soon the three were standing shoulder to shoulder upon the trapdoors repeating the prayers of the priests standing nearby. The nooses, of four-strand hemp rope, hung from a strong crossbeam just above their heads. Martin shook Rudge by the hand. The *Carlisle Journal* noted that Martin 'was a man of great nerve and power of self-restraint, and none of the three went to the gallows with such a firm determination'.

White hoods were placed over their heads. As de Crespigny strapped their legs, Berry fastened the nooses. As the hangman prepared to draw the bolt, Baker's plaintive, broken voice was heard to say 'Nellie, keep straight! I die an innocent man, but I forgive everybody.'

The drop fell, leaving the men dangling inside the pit. Martin and Baker had plummeted through the floor of the scaffold, but Rudge's head, hooded in the noose, remained obstinately above it, as if arrogantly taunting his tormentors from beyond death's great divide. At 12st 10lbs he was the heaviest of the three, and was given only a four feet drop. Martin was allowed six feet and Baker six and a half. This meant that the beam did not have to bear the strain of their combined weights instantaneously.

A crowd of between two and three thousand people had gathered in the streets, bringing traffic to a standstill. A few minutes after 8 am a cry went up as the black flag was hoisted above the prison entrance. Not long afterwards James Berry, whose appetite had evidently not been affected by the proceedings, went over to the County Hotel to have breakfast. He was recognized by patrons outraged that the common hangman, 'reeking from the gallows', should share the coffee room with them. Berry rounded on one protestor, an elderly military man, and threatened to give him a 'six-foot drop and a squeeze'. The hotel manager explained that he could not prevent Berry, a recognized officer of the law, from using the facilities. It was ironic that, although the police superintendent, the prosecuting barrister or the judge who had condemned the men to death would have been welcomed at any table in the hotel, the individual who had put that sentence into effect was treated as a pariah.

James Berry had further executions scheduled for the following Tuesday, Wednesday and Thursday – a total of seven people put to death in four days. To him it was merely a job, but one of the two press representatives at the execution, John Burgess of the *Carlisle Patriot*, was so affected by the ghastly ordeal of witnessing this ritual killing that he left his family for three days and nights afterwards to walk alone on the fells around Caldbeck on the edge of the Lake District.[19]

At II am the inquest began. After being sworn in, the jury viewed the bodies, which lay in coffins in the room where the men had been hanged. Berry, as we have seen, had in 1885 given Robert Goodale too long a drop, causing his head to be ripped off by the impact. Occasionally the opposite occurred, with people allowed too short a drop, with the consequence that they remained alive and struggling for some time, even minutes, after the plunge through the trap. This may have happened to Baker, as the rope from which he was suspended had been seen to vibrate for a short while. The second journalist present, William Steel of the *Carlisle Journal*, was shocked to see that 'Baker's face was swollen, his eyes were only half closed, and his appearance was ghastly'.

The stone to Rudge, Martin and Baker in Carlisle Cemetery. *Brian Norman*

The stomachs of the onlookers were further put to the test when Dr Henry Lediard stated that Rudge had asked several times for blood-sucking leeches to be put on his head, as he thought he was suffering from 'an overflow of blood'. Rudge was apparently convinced that there was something wrong with his brain, and wanted Lediard to cut open his skull after the execution and examine it. Permission for this peculiar post-mortem was, however, refused. That evening the bodies of Rudge, Martin and Baker were buried by lantern-light against the prison wall.

Back in Bethnal Green, James Baker's heartbroken parents kept the shutters of their furniture shop in Virginia Row firmly closed for a time, as related in *East End Underworld*, Raphael Samuel's biography of Arthur Harding. Baker's father Thomas died in 1889 at the age of 57, and the census returns of 1891 and 1901 show that the widowed Ellen Baker continued to run the business with the assistance of two of her daughters. Ellen lived until 1911, when she passed away at the age of 79.

Now that Rudge, Martin and Baker had paid the ultimate penalty, attention turned towards the capture of the mysterious Fourth Man. Witnesses agreed on his existence, confirmed by the discovery of the discarded light-coloured overcoat in the River Eden. According to the *Carlisle Patriot*, Martin had stated that they had accidentally met the man in an eating-house in Longtown before the Netherby robbery. Martin, it seems, knew him of old – he was an ex-convict, and carried a revolver. On hearing that the man intended to walk to Carlisle later that evening, Martin asked him to meet them on the outskirts of Longtown at 8.30 pm so that he could show them the way. The man, Martin claimed, was not aware of the intended robbery.

The police lost no time in pulling in likely suspects, but could not sustain a case against any of them. Two, oddly enough, also had the surname Baker. One was William Baker, a local man with a long criminal record. The other gave his name as James Baker, but was known to use the aliases Smith and Johnstone. He was known as 'One-Armed Jim' because he had lost a hand, in place of which he used an iron hook. Arrested in London, he was brought up to Carlisle by Chief Inspector Shore, accompanied by Chief Inspector Frederick Abberline (who would lead the Jack the Ripper investigation in 1888). Both these suspects were rearrested several times in the following months, but key witnesses failed to single them out in identity parades and charges were not brought against them.

Many years later a story circulated identifying the Fourth Man with a Mr Summers, who claimed to be a head painter with Maples, the London furniture manufacturers.[20] Summers had apparently been seen jumping from a train waiting at a signal near the village of Kirkpatrick Fleming, about three miles north-west of Gretna. After washing his face in a stream he obtained some breakfast at a nearby cottage, explaining he had lost his luggage and overcoat. Some years later, the same man, now calling himself Parker, fell seriously ill while working on the Canadian Pacific Railway. When close to death, he apparently confessed that he had been the Fourth Man in the Netherby affair. He stated that, although he had been a thief, and not averse to using violence, he drew the line at murder. Having witnessed his companions brutally attacking the policemen who got in their way, he realized they would stop at nothing, and had left them at the first opportunity.

The family of Joseph Byrnes

Three years after the murder of Byrnes, his widow Eleanor married William Casson Holmes, a 20-year-old railway clerk. The couple initially lived at Whitehaven until William was appointed station-master at Haverbrack in Westmorland. By 1901 Eleanor and her new husband had three children, Isabella, William and Wilfrid Holmes, in addition to the four from her first marriage.

Eleanor had doubtless been present at the unveiling of a memorial to Joseph Byrnes set into the wall at the spot where he had been killed at Plumpton. It was inscribed: *Do or die | Here Constable Joseph Byrnes | fell on the night of Oct 25 1885 | Shot by the three Netherby burglars | whom he single handedly endeavoured | to arrest.*

If there had also been a wooden marker or cross on his actual grave at Penrith Cemetery, it must have rotted away over the years, for by the twenty-first century the spot was unmarked. Brian Parnaby, a great-nephew of Byrnes, researched its location, and

The memorial marking the spot where the mortally wounded PC Byrnes was thrown over the wall.
Brian Norman

the Cumbria Police Federation sponsored an impressive new stone unveiled in 2006, exactly 121 years to the day after the murder.

Christopher Gaddes

His role in the arrest of Rudge, Martin and Baker must have given Gaddes a taste for thwarting crime. In April 1887, eighteen months after the dramatic capture, he resigned from his post as a goods guard for the London & North Western Railway and became a police constable. He was stationed at Whitehaven, and in 1891 was living at 5 Michael Street with his wife Catherine and children Bessie and Sidney. His new career was only to last five years, however. Gaddes resigned in March 1892, and by the time of the 1901 census was running a grocery business at Swan Street in his native Longtown.

The Grahams of Netherby Hall

Perhaps the Graham family at nearby Netherby Hall patronized the Gaddes shop from time to time in recognition of his part in the capture of the burglars. Sir Frederick Graham died on 8 March 1888 aged 67 at his London home in Park Lane, and was brought back to Longtown for burial in the family vault at St Michael's Parish Church. His widow Lady Hermione was laid beside him in April 1909 after her death at the age of 77.

In his *Foul Deeds and Suspicious Deaths in and around Carlisle*, Ian Ashbridge writes that the Netherby case 'continued to grip the imagination of the public. It was a popular local play as late as 1938.' The revolvers and the bullet that killed PC Byrnes now form part of the collection of the Tullie House Museum in Carlisle. Wax models of Rudge, Martin and Baker were created for display at the Chamber of Horrors at Madame Tussaud's in London. Sir Charles Graham, great-grandson of Sir Frederick and Lady Hermione, vividly remembered being taken to see the figures as a child. Unfortunately they were destroyed in a Second World War air raid. As for the murderers themselves, Carlisle Gaol burial ground was not destined to be their final resting place. The prison was closed in 1922 and its demolition complete by 1931. The remains of executed prisoners were exhumed and reburied in Carlisle Cemetery, and a plaque marks the spot where Rudge, Martin and Baker now lie.

16

'But They Can Receive'

We have seen that the Justices of the Peace for Essex, the Beacontree Division and the Liberty of Havering had combined to offer a reward of £250 for information leading to the conviction of the murderer of Thomas Simmons. The guilty verdict against James Adams and his subsequent execution led, as would be expected, to a number of applications from people claiming to have brought about his capture. The magistrates and the Essex Chief Constable, Major William Poyntz, eventually decided to split the £250 among those who had each, in their opinion, contributed towards the successful prosecution of Adams. Elizabeth Salmon, the optician's wife, received a letter offering her £5, which she agreed to accept. Another fell on the doormat of the house in Clapham where Edward Baxter, the pawnbroker's assistant, lived with his parents. Baxter was far from happy to read that he would be awarded £50. Had he not made the greatest contribution by tipping off the police that Adams had entered his shop, and put himself in danger by keeping the villain talking until the officers arrived? Baxter obtained a lawyer, and took legal action against the justices to claim the entire £250.

On 3 August 1886 the case was heard at the Queen's Bench before Mr Justice Denman, son of the former Lord Chief Justice Lord Denman. Lawyers for both sides agreed that the wording of offer of the reward meant that only one person could justly lay claim to it. But who should that person be? Baxter, as the plaintiff in the case, was first to give evidence. He declared that, although the police had called many times about the matter, it had been his own idea to send a message to Platt Street Police Station when Adams appeared. According to the *Essex Times*, Baxter went on to say that 'Superintendent Dobson informed me that if I could tell where [Adams] was or lay my hands upon him he would take me to the bank – Coutts, I think – and give me £100 without bringing my name into the affair in any shape or form.'

For the defence, barristers representing the justices asserted that it was not Baxter, but Detective Sergeant William Rolfe who had played the major role in the capture. Rolfe himself was then called, and stated that he had told the pawn shop staff that officers at Platt Street were ready to respond as soon as they received a message that Adams was in the shop. Rolfe was asked whether he had put in for the reward.

'I do not claim any reward. The police are not allowed to claim', he answered; then added 'But they can receive.' When the resulting laughter had subsided, he stated that 'In this case the Commissioners were asked if they would allow me to receive anything and they said they would allow me to receive any sum the authorities felt disposed to give.'

In his summing-up, Mr Justice Denman declared that 'these cases were very difficult to decide, owing to the vague wording generally used in the placards offering rewards, and he expressed a strong opinion that these offerings of rewards ought to be abolished altogether'. He urged counsel for both sides not to hold out for 'winner takes all', but to agree on a division of the sum between Baxter and Rolfe. According to the *Essex Times*, the judge said that

> it seemed a pity that two persons so equally meritorious as Baxter and Rolfe should have come to the question which in point of law was entitled to receive a reward for meritorious services, because he could not for a moment doubt that both of these men had behaved extremely well. The plaintiff most courageously assisted in the capture of a man who was a dangerous murderer, and the detective discharged his duty with great discretion and zeal and great diligence in tracing the man as far as he could from place to place and in getting such information as would likely ultimately lead to his detection and conviction.

The legal teams would not budge, however, so the members of the jury were sent out to confer. After being absent an hour they sent a message asking if a majority verdict would be accepted. The counsel on both sides having agreed to this, the jury returned and announced that the majority were for the plaintiff, Mr Baxter. He would be given £250, and Rolfe would leave with nothing. The *Essex Times* indignantly told its readers that:

> Mr Baxter is probably the only man living who is thoroughly satisfied with the result of the action brought by him . . . He certainly gave very valuable help in securing the apprehension of Menson [sic], alias Adams, alias Lee, a most desperate and dangerous criminal, whose latest murder was the slaying of Inspector Simmons . . . But Sergeant Rolfe took the first and the most important step in coming to the right conclusion that Menson was the man to seek. It was by Rolfe's patient interpretation of slight indications and his patient following out of obscure clues that he was led to paying a visit to Baxter . . . It is not easy to see on what ground the majority of the jury . . . came to the conclusion that Baxter was the one person entitled to the reward . . .

William Rolfe, as we have seen, had been a boot and shoe maker before entering the Metropolitan Police in 1876, and had kept many acquaintances from his former line of work. One of these was Harry James Frith, who had netted the considerable fortune of almost £10,000 from a boot and shoe manufacturing and retailing business based at Westminster Bridge Road, Lambeth, with sub-branches in Chelsea and Clapham. In the summer of 1886 Frith, aged only 35, lay dying of tuberculosis. He was separated from his wife and had custody of their young children Ettie, Rose and Harry.

On 17 June Frith made his will, naming William Rolfe as one of the executors and asking him to become guardian of the Frith children. Rolfe was also offered the position of general manager of Frith's business. It came with a salary of £200 per annum, a profit-related bonus, and rent-free accommodation at the main premises. On Friday 15 October Harry Frith died at Guy's Hospital, and Rolfe had to decide whether to accept the position offered to him in the will.

He immediately wrote his letter of resignation, which must have come as a great disappointment to his colleagues and superiors. This terse entry appears in the Police Orders: 'Resigned: 60402 Rolfe, Police Sergeant CID, H-division. Pay to 17th October'. No doubt Rolfe was aggrieved at the outcome of the Simmons reward case, and he obviously felt a sense of obligation towards the wishes of his friend. The offer of managership of a thriving business on such generous terms was perhaps too good to refuse.

Rolfe, his wife Eliza and their children packed up and left their home at 8 Redman Row, Mile End, and moved across the Thames to Westminster Bridge Road. The 1891 census shows the two eldest Rolfe sons, 20-year-old George and Thomas, 18, now working for their father as shop assistants. By 1901 Rolfe had moved to new business premises at nearby 76 York Road. It was here that he died, aged 54, on 1 July 1902. His son George registered the death the following day, the cause being given as Chronic Bulbar Paralysis.

Rolfe's fellow detective George Mellish was to have a much longer career in the Metropolitan Police. Eventually promoted to detective inspector, he retired 16 August 1902 after serving for thirty-four years and ninety-one days. An article in the *Police Review* describes the gifts presented to him, including a 'massive tea and coffee service by the Detective Inspectors of the Metropolitan Police' and 'a watch and chain from his K Division colleagues', together with a 'large photographic group, framed in oak, of the Detective Officers of the K Division'. Mellish did not plan a life of leisure on his £161 15s 2d per annum pension. Less than two weeks later he was sailing to Western Australia on board the *Omrah* to start a new job as head of the Detective Department of the Perth Police Force. Mellish only remained in Australia for two years, resigning his post in October 1904. He immediately returned to England, where he lived until his death at the age of 99 in 1947.

Let's now look at the later lives of those who were affected by the murder of Thomas Simmons and its aftermath.

Simmons's Wife and Children

As we have seen, Thomas Simmons had privately rented Cavendish Villa in South Street, Romford, and after his death his widow Mary Ann chose to remain there. She was joined by her sister and brother-in-law Ellen and Alfred Oxley. Her children Emily and Willie soon grew to adulthood. There must have been great excitement when Emily announced her engagement to George Samuel Mather, a solicitor and magistrates' clerk who had assisted Thomas Shekell Haynes at Romford before becoming clerk to the East Ham justices. The couple married on 12 July 1898 at the Emmanuel Church in Forest Gate. Mrs Simmons was not to lose her daughter's company, however, as the newlyweds settled in a house named Glenville, at 58 Western Road, just a few minutes' walk from Cavendish Villa.

By the time of the 1901 census Emily's younger brother William, aged 27, was still living at home and employed as a clerk in a paper mill. In later years, however, he was to turn his back on his home town and comfortable office job. He moved to Balham in South London and worked as a billiard marker or scorekeeper in billiard halls. On 10 July 1910 William died aged only 36 at the Union Infirmary, St John's Hill, Wandsworth. The principal cause of death was certified as Tabes Dorsalis. William's uncle Alfred Oxley arranged for the young man's body to be brought back to Romford, where he was buried alongside his father at Crow Lane Cemetery on 15 July 1910.

Seven years later the family was plunged into grief once more with the death of William's sister Emily. She passed away aged 48 in Victoria Cottage Hospital, Romford, on 23 April 1917, after an operation for ovarian cancer. Her funeral took place at Crow Lane Cemetery four days later, the mourners including the Mayor and Mayoress of East Ham. Emily's husband George Mather later remarried and moved to Westcliff-on-Sea. When he died in April 1929 his body was buried alongside Emily at Crow Lane.

Mary Ann Simmons had now lost both her children, and as both had been childless the direct line of descent from Thomas Simmons died out. As the years flowed by Mrs Simmons remained at Cavendish Villa with the Oxleys, familiarly known as Nell and Alf, while the character of South Street changed around them.

The 1890s Romford Police Station. Part of the house in which Mrs Simmons still lived can be seen on the right. *Essex Police Museum*

The clatter of horse-drawn traffic gave way to the roar of the motor engine. Surrounding buildings altered too; only the Market Place end of South Street had formerly been devoted to shops, but they gradually spread southwards towards the railway station. A surprising development had occurred back in the early 1890s. The decision had at last been made to provide a purpose-built police station in place of the inadequate office inside the old Court House. What must Mrs Simmons's feelings have been on learning that it would be built next door to her home? The new police station was opened in 1894, and remained in use until 1965.

On 3 September 1925 Mary Ann Simmons passed away at home aged 81 from the effects of an umbilical hernia. Her death made the headlines in local newspapers, many readers vividly remembering the sensational events of forty years before. 'Echo of a Romford tragedy: death of Mrs Simmons', proclaimed the *Barking Advertiser*, while the front page of the *Essex Times* declared: 'Murder drama recalled'. Four days later Mary Ann was buried alongside Thomas and William. The numerous wreaths included one reading 'With deepest sympathy from the Romford Division of Police', and Romford's current inspector, A E Denny, was one

Detail of a 1954 plan showing the police station on the left and the Romford Arcade which was built on the site of the Simmons house. *London Borough of Havering Local Studies*

of a large contingent of police officers at the funeral. Alfred Marden is not reported as attending, although his brother Howard, a retired police sergeant, was present. Family mourners included Mary Ann's sisters Mrs Robinson, Mrs Stringer and Mrs Oxley, and her brothers Edward, John and Frederick Jennings.

After Mary Ann's death, Ellen and Alfred Oxley moved to 87 Victoria Road where they lived with their niece Irene Jeffries, daughter of Ellen's sister Isabella Jennings. The Oxleys did not long outlive Mary Ann, for both died at home in 1929. Ellen succumbed to heart disease on 25 February aged 80, and Alfred followed aged 82 on 22 October after suffering cirrhosis of the liver.

Simmons's Police Colleagues

Alfred Marden

In the summer of 1885, not long after the murder of Simmons and its aftermath, Alfred Marden was able to turn his thoughts to a happier topic. On 7 September he was married to 25-year-old Mary Weekes Newberry at Sidmouth in South Devon. Mary, born in Dorset but working as a servant in London, was the daughter of a retired coastguard.

Marden became an acting sergeant in 1888 and transferred to Prittlewell, near Southend. He and Mary appear there on the 1891 census at 4 Sussex Terrace, Alexandra Street, with their sons Sidney Thomas, 4, and Alfred aged 1. Marden's aptitude for detective work was displayed three years later after the body of a young pregnant woman named Florrie Dennis was found shot in the head at Prittlewell. Marden played a vital part in the capture of her killer, James Canham Read. In March 1900 he was appointed detective sergeant and transferred back to

Romford. He and Mary settled with their family, now comprising four sons and a daughter, in Victoria Road, close to where Thomas Simmons had lived three decades before. In 1901, by a strange twist of fate, Marden was appointed to Simmons's old job as inspector at Romford. He probably remained in close touch with Mary Ann Simmons who, of course, now lived next door to the police station.

Marden investigated several notable murder cases during his career, the most high-profile of which was the so-called Moat Farm Murder. This resulted in the execution of Samuel Herbert Dougal in 1903 for killing Camille Holland at Clavering. Later that year Marden was appointed superintendent of the Brentwood Division. Romford's inhabitants gave him a farewell gift of a gold watch, 'in recognition of conspicuous ability and zealous performance of duty'.

In April 1911, at the age of 48, Marden reached the pinnacle of his career when he became superintendent of the Southend Division, the largest in the county. However, his reputation was to crash in flames not long afterwards. Martyn Lockwood recounts in his essay *The Rise and Fall of Alfred John Marden* how in 1912 an internal inquiry found Marden guilty of various offences extending back to 1903. They included illegally questioning prisoners, lying, swearing and not showing proper respect to the Chief Constable. Marden was demoted from superintendent to inspector, and allowed to retire soon afterwards.

Like many ex-policemen Marden then became a private investigator, but ran into trouble again in 1920. In November that year he was employed by a Miss Wakefield, who alleged that a certain Charles Horace Suttling of The Avenue, Purfleet, was the father of her illegitimate child. Marden, it seems, confronted Suttling at his home one evening with 'I am an inspector of police and I want to speak to you.' After failing to persuade the man to admit paternity of the child, Marden told him 'I shall have to take you to the station'. He then grabbed Suttling's arm and led him out of the house without even allowing him to put his coat on. Still the man denied the accusation, so Marden eventually let him go.

The outcome was that Marden was summoned to appear before the Grays magistrates charged with impersonating a police officer. The *Essex Times* printed a full report. Charles Suttling's evidence was supported by his sister and brother-in-law who had been present during the incident. Marden denied he had told Suttling he was a police inspector, and claimed he had mentioned a railway station, not a police station. The chairman of magistrates announced that they were in no doubt that Marden was guilty, and would levy a fine of £5 plus costs. A further charge of assaulting Charles Suttling was not proceeded with. It was an ignominious end to a remarkable career. On Christmas Eve 1933 Marden died aged 70 at his home in Princes Street, Southend.

Sergeant George Chase

Chase, as we have seen, had joined the force the same day as Thomas Simmons, and had been on duty at Romford Police Station when Edward Matthews had leapt out of the horse and trap with the dreadful news of the shooting. Chase eventually became an inspector at Rochford, and an amusing anecdote describes how he once spotted two sleeping figures behind the Rose and Crown. Believing they were vagrants, Chase tried to turn one of the figures over with the toecap of his boot, but, writes Lynn Tait in her article *The Boobing Bobby*, 'Well, how was he to know that one of the prone shadows was a travelling showman and that the other, the shadow he was now trying to turn, was the fellow's performing grizzly bear? Inspector Chase had to free himself from the creature's hairy grip before fleeing into the night.' Chase retired in March 1902, and continued to live at Rochford until his death aged 68 in 1914.

Superintendent John Dobson

Dobson, as we have seen, worked closely with Simmons from the late 1870s onwards, and played a leading role in the investigation into his murder. Dobson retired in February 1893 with a pension of £116 13s 4d per annum, and settled down to live in Shenfield, just outside Brentwood, with his wife Edith and young family. He died aged 71 in 1911.

Frederick Wilderspin

It was Wilderspin who had seen the three men get off the train at Rainham Station on 20 January 1885. He thus played a vital part in setting off the chain of events which culminated in the murder of Simmons. Wilderspin continued to serve as a constable at Dagenham, and at the time of the 1891 census was living at 4 Station Road with his wife Susannah and 6-year-old daughter Ettie, who had lost an eye as the result of an accident. Sadly,

George Samuel Chase in later life.
Essex Police Museum

Wilderspin only had a few more years to live. He died of tuberculosis 18 April 1894 aged 44, and was buried four days later in the parish churchyard. Wilderspin's wife and daughter ran a sweet shop in Church Street, Dagenham, before dying within four months of each other in 1917.

David Dredge

So close a brush with the hangman must have had a sobering effect, even on a man with the wayward temperament of David Dredge. After serving his twelve-month sentence with hard labour for threatening Marden with a gun, Dredge seems to have settled back into the modest lifestyle of a hay binder. In the 1890s he set up home with a much younger woman named Martha Smee, whose husband James was serving ten years' penal servitude for stealing two bullocks. Dredge continued to father children with Martha until he was well into his sixties. By the time of the 1901 census James Smee had been freed, but his wife was still living with Dredge at Albion Street in Romford. Martha was listed as Mrs Dredge, although it seems unlikely that the couple ever married.

Dredge and Martha later moved to 18 Wolseley Road, Rush Green, just a stone's throw from Crow Lane Cemetery where Thomas Simmons lay buried. Dredge passed away at his home aged 79 on 12 June 1913. The cause of death was given as 'senility and cardiac arrest'. Martha died aged 60 in April 1921 and was buried in the same grave. Their home in Wolseley Road has now been demolished and replaced by a modern dwelling, but similar properties remain elsewhere in the road.

Philip Stern

Philip Stern, who had spared no effort in defending David Dredge, returned to his native Jamaica in 1893 on health grounds but continued to practise as both a barrister and solicitor. He was regarded as the island's leading criminal lawyer, with unrivalled skills in cross-examination. Stern took up the cases of many anti-establishment figures, such as the black revivalist preacher Alexander Bedward who had been arrested for sedition.

In the mid-1890s Philip Stern entered both local and national politics. He briefly represented the Parish of St Catherine in the Legislative Council (Jamaica's parliament) in 1895, and then represented Kingston from January 1896 to July 1908. He was also three times Mayor of Kingston. After his retirement from the Legislative Council, he held the post of clerk to the council until 1924. He had the distinction of being appointed KC (King's Counsel) in 1913. Philip Stern died at his home of Neil's Court, Waterloo Road, Kingston, on 14 September 1933, and was buried in the Orange Street Jewish Cemetery the following day.

The Family of James Adams

Unfortunately little is known of the subsequent life of Adams's wife Charlotte, left with four young children after his execution in 1885. By the time of the 1891 census her elder son George Manson, aged 11, had been consigned to St Mary's Orphanage, Heston. Ten years later the younger son, James, born just days before his father's arrest, was living with his uncle William Kitchen in Islington and working as a labourer.

The Eye-Witnesses to the Shooting

Edward Matthews remained in Romford, and at the time of the 1901 census was living at Waterloo Road and working as a carman, carrying out deliveries in a horse and cart for Romford Urban District Council. He died aged 82 in December 1927 and was buried at Crow Lane Cemetery.

David Kemp continued to live in Brazier's Yard, just off the High Street, until his death at the age of 76. He too was buried at Crow Lane, on 26 April 1891.

Their companion in witnessing the murder, John Sawkins, is difficult to trace, but he may possibly be identified with a labourer of the same name who died in Romford Union Workhouse aged 50 and was buried at Crow Lane on 6 June 1898.

The Chairman of the Romford Magistrates: Joseph Fry

Mr Fry died on Christmas Day 1896 aged 87 and was buried in St Andrew's churchyard in Hornchurch on 31 December. He had lived at Fairkytes, Hornchurch, for just under thirty years, and according to the *Essex Review* 'he was always ready to aid any project having for its object the well-being of the community amongst whom he lived'. Mr Fry had worked tirelessly as chairman of the Romford magistrates until only a year before his death. Henry Shekell Haynes, the magistrates' clerk, stated that: 'For some 25 years he had had the honour and pleasure of Mr Fry's society, and he felt that they had lost in him, not only a man of public business, but many of them a very dear friend.'

The Coroner: Henry Shekell Haynes

Less than three years after paying tribute to Mr Fry, Henry Haynes himself passed away on 2 June 1899 at his home at New Place, Upminster, at the age of 57. He left a widow Caroline and five children. Romford solicitor Mr J W Atkinson declared that 'Probably, a more sound lawyer or a more polished gentleman had never sat at the Clerk's desk'. Casting his mind back, perhaps, to the fiery confrontation between Haynes and Philip Stern, Mr Atkinson added: 'Mr Haynes might, perhaps, have been a little hasty at times; but all of them were liable to be that; but a friendship with Mr Haynes extending over 20 years had convinced him that a kinder heart had never beat beneath a human breast.'

Dr Alfred Wright

Dr Wright, who as a young man had fought so hard to save the life of Thomas Simmons, was to become a prominent figure in the Romford area. He was a prime mover in the founding of the Victoria Cottage Hospital, built to commemorate the Golden Jubilee of Queen Victoria in 1887. He also became a justice of the peace and deputy chairman of the Romford magistrates. Dr Wright left his South Street home, The Lodge, and moved to a house in Main Road which he named Mountsorrel after his Leicestershire birthplace. His son Dr Eric Alfred Wright joined him in the medical practice until he volunteered to serve with the Royal Army Medical Corps in the First World War. Eric was tragically killed in Alexandria in 1915 aged 36, and a plaque to his memory was placed inside St Edward's Church. Alfred Wright died at his home aged 81 on 29 January 1921. The current chairman of the local magistrates declared that Dr Wright 'had done great work in Romford . . . The life he had led as a doctor and as a magistrate would be a great example to the rising generation', while the *Romford Times* remembered his 'extremely kind nature'. Dr Wright was buried at Crow Lane Cemetery, and four years later his widow Elizabeth Sarah was interred with him.

The Hangman: James Berry

Berry resigned from his post in 1891 at the age of 39 after hanging more than 130 people. The following year he published his autobiography, *My Experiences as an Executioner*. Berry tried his hand at a succession of futile alternative occupations before reapplying for the executioner's job in 1902. He was turned down. Berry became increasingly depressed and even suicidal, before undergoing a religious conversion and adopting a new career as a touring evangelical preacher. He died aged 61 in 1913.

The Hangman's Assistant: Sir Claude de Crespigny

Sir Claude forged a remarkable reputation in typical Victorian fashion as a sportsman and adventurer, setting many records. In 1883 he had become the first man to cross the North Sea in a balloon, and six years later he was the first European to swim the Nile rapids. He continued his steeplechasing career until the age of 67, and afterwards, according to the *Dictionary of National Biography*, 'devoted himself to the more leisurely pursuits, as he saw them, of sailing, swimming, high diving and long-distance walking'. On his death in June 1935 aged 88 he was interred in a mausoleum in the grounds of his home, Champion Lodge near Maldon, but was reburied in the 1950s in St Andrew's churchyard, Hatfield Peverel.

Romford in the Present Day

If Thomas Simmons could return to Romford now, he would find very little surviving of the town that he knew. Cavendish Villa, his house in South Street, was demolished not long after Mary Ann's death. In its place rose the town's first covered shopping area, the art deco-style Romford Arcade. Stores included Craddocks, offering stationery, china and fancy goods, and Norman Stanley, which specialized in radio accessories. A big draw for the Arcade in the 1960s was Wells Music Stores, in which teenagers could sample the latest hits in the listening booths. The Arcade in its turn has also gone, but the name survives in Arcade Place, which links South Street with the Brewery shopping complex. A well-known location in Arcade Place is the Romford Snooker Centre, formerly the Luciania, where six-times world champion Steve Davis learnt his trade.

Simmons would also notice the absence of the Congregational Church, demolished in 1965. The county court on the opposite side of South Street, where Adams and Dredge were brought before the magistrates, was pulled down after a new court was built behind the police station in South Street in 1931. On the creation of the London Borough of Havering in 1965, a new police station and court house were built in Main Road and the old buildings made way for more shops. Moving on to the Market Place, the returning Simmons would discover that the old Court House, his place of work for so many years, has also been swept away. After the departure of the police it housed council offices until its demolition in the 1930s.

The site of the Simmons house today. *Authors' collection*

By contrast St Andrew's Church, where Simmons and Mary Ann were married in 1868, still stands, as does St Edward's Church in the Market Place. The Golden Lion still occupies its 500-year-old site on the corner of the High Street and North Street. In a quiet nook around the corner, facing the former location of the old Court House, the Lamb sits where it has done since the fire of 1852 destroyed its predecessor. The original Ind Coope Brewery buildings in the High Street have also survived, although beer production ceased in February 1993. The site has largely been converted to residential use, and will also house the new Havering Museum, due to open in late 2009.

The actual scene of the shooting of Simmons on that January afternoon over 120 years ago is in many respects unchanged. One can easily follow in the wheeltracks of Simmons and Marden as they pursued Dredge and his companions, beginning at what is now the Albion pub, close to the Dovers Corner roundabout. The Cherry Tree (rebuilt and enlarged) still stands at the crossroads where Simmons turned right into South End Road. The third turning on the left, about 500 metres from the Cherry Tree, is Ford Lane. We can follow Simmons into this road and up to the junction of Rainham Road (now Upper Rainham Road) where he turned right. This section still retains some of the atmosphere of a country lane. As it winds northwards, the

The sewage farm no longer exists, but this modern gate in Upper Rainham Road is on the site of the old entrance through which the gunmen escaped. *Authors' collection*

impressive bulk of Bretons House comes into view amidst open land to the left.

Bretons is currently an Outdoor Recreation Centre for the London Borough of Havering. We pass its entrance on the left, continuing to follow the road as it bends first to the left then to the right. As the railway bridge comes into view, we are at the point where Simmons made the fatal decision to confront the two men. The sewage works has now gone, having closed in 1969. To our left stands a modern gate, marking the spot where the gunman and his accomplice squeezed through the gap next to the old gate and made their escape across the fields towards Dagenham. This stretch of land, over which the mortally wounded Simmons joined the pursuit, is still open space, which on the Dagenham side of the river becomes Eastbrookend Country Park.

Conclusion: 'The Last Patrol'

The investigating police officers and the Old Bailey judge were certain that the right man, James Adams, was convicted and hanged for the killing of Thomas Simmons. Detective Sergeant Rolfe, who led the murder hunt, firmly believed that Adams pulled the trigger and that John Martin had been his accomplice. Yet the question still lingers – does the available evidence point incontrovertibly to Adams being the gunman? There seems to be no doubt that he was at the scene. His defence barrister made no attempt to establish an alibi. Yet Adams continued to deny responsibility for the actual shooting, even upon the scaffold, where he declared 'I die an innocent man. Remember that!'

The main sticking point is the question of the gunman's height. He was dubbed 'the Tall Man' by the press. We have the witness statement of Simmons himself, in which he declared that the man was 'tall, six feet or so'. Prison records reveal that Adams was only 5 feet $8^{1}/2$ inches. Simmons himself was 5 feet 9 inches, and it seems odd that he should so mistake the height of a man he had encountered at very close quarters. Of the other witnesses, Frederick Wilderspin had the best view of the three suspects, having watched them walk past him on the platform at Rainham. Wilderspin stated repeatedly, even at the Old Bailey trial itself, that Adams was *not* the tallest of the three. Alfred Marden, however, maintained that Adams was the gunman, although Marden had been a full sixty yards from the scene, and daylight was fading fast. The sewage farm labourers, Matthews, Kemp and Sawkins, who were closest to the actual shooting, didn't pick out anybody from the identity parade. Nor did they identify Adams when he stood in the dock at the magistrates' court hearings and at the Old Bailey.

The fascinating science of ballistics, which matches the ineradicable characteristics left by rifling grooves on a bullet to the pistol from which it was fired, was not perfected until 1889. There was, therefore, in 1885 no means of proving that the revolver which Adams tried to pawn was, in fact, the murder weapon. The jury at his trial could only be informed that bullets found in his possession, and in the pocket of the overcoat, were 'similar' to the one which had killed Inspector Simmons. In 1885 even basic fingerprinting techniques had not yet been developed, and we can now of course make use of DNA samples from bloodstains, hairs and fibres of clothing to link individuals to a crime scene.

James Adams had not even met his defence barrister John Peter Grain before the trial. If Mr Grain had had longer to prepare his defence he may have been better able to convey to the jury the holes in the evidence. For a murder trial to last only two days would be unthinkable now.

So, how tall was John Martin? Unfortunately, prison records do not provide a definite height for him. Anthony Rudge, though, is recorded in the Newgate registers of 1870 (under his real name, William Fennell) as being 5 feet 9 inches. After the arrest of Martin and Rudge, the *Carlisle Journal* stated that Martin 'is a man of taller and more slender build' than Rudge. Martin must, therefore, have been taller than both Adams and Simmons. As we have seen, he confessed to the murder of Joseph Byrnes shortly before his execution. If he shot Byrnes in cold blood attempting to make his escape, then he was more than capable of killing Simmons too.

The overcoat dropped by the gunman during the pursuit contained the spectacles case that was traced convincingly back to Adams. Yet had he been wearing the coat at the time? We have seen that when Rudge, Martin and Baker were on the run in Cumberland, they swopped coats and hats in order to confuse witnesses and throw doubt on identification. Is it possible that Adams and Martin had also done this after first being seen by Simmons and Marden?

If Martin was indeed the gunman, then by throwing off the coat during the flight he was helping to condemn his accomplice to death. And, assuming that Adams had not killed Simmons, what must his predicament have been? Did he feel bound to keep silent about Martin's involvement because of the code of 'Honour amongst Thieves'? Or was he ever tempted to betray his comrade in the hope of saving his own life?

The Victorian legal system may well, however, have viewed this whole argument about who pulled the trigger as irrelevant. If a group of criminals went armed with deadly weapons in a common purpose, then they were seen as equally guilty. A more modern example of this view happened in 1953, when 19-year-old Derek Bentley was hanged for the murder of PC Sidney Miles although it was not disputed that Christopher Craig, 16, had actually fired the gun.

The murder of Inspector Simmons made national headlines at the time. Local retailers even offered souvenirs in the shape of memorial cards headed 'The Last Patrol. Inspector Simmons shot by burglars January 20 1885.' Yet by the 1990s the crime had slipped from public view to such an extent that Fred Feather, in *The Amateur Hangman*, described it as 'possibly the most obscure of all the murders of Essex policemen'.

Two other notorious police killings took place nearby. In 1846 PC George Clark was brutally murdered in Dagenham. The 150th anniversary of the crime was marked by a programme of events including the planting of a memorial tree in

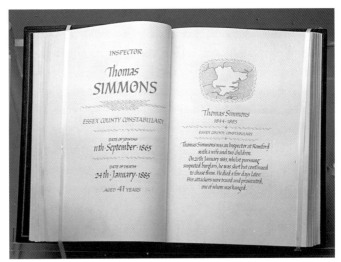

Pages from the Essex
Police Roll of Honour
commemorating
Thomas Simmons.
*Essex Police
Museum*

Eastbrookend Country Park. In 1927 PC George Gutteridge was shot dead on a country road in Stapleford Abbotts, north of Romford. There is a memorial at the scene, and a short stretch of the highway itself has been named Gutteridge Lane.

By contrast, the death of Inspector Thomas Simmons seems to have been generally overlooked in the Romford area. His name is of course included in the Essex Police's Book of Remembrance and Roll of Honour, both of which are on

A late nineteenth-century view of Romford Market looking west. The Court House where Simmons served can be seen in the centre background. *London Borough of Havering Local Studies*

view at the force's headquarters at Chelmsford. Simmons is also listed on the National Police Memorial in the Mall, unveiled by the Queen in April 2005. His grave in Crow Lane Cemetery is cared for by the Essex Police Memorial Trust, but there is at present nothing to mark the spot in Upper Rainham Road where he was shot. It is hoped that a memorial will be placed at or close to the scene in time for the 125th anniversary of his murder in January 2010.

Romford is greatly changed now, but the story of Thomas Simmons opens a window for us back into the 1880s. We have walked with him around the town and met the inhabitants. It is now time to leave Simmons, his family and police colleagues and return to the twenty-first century. Amidst the present whirlwind of change, Romford Market has remained a constant, and stalls are still put up each Wednesday as they have been since 1247. The animals have gone now – the last cattle market was held in 1958 – but Simmons would, no doubt, still feel at home here, amongst the shouts and calls of the stall-holders and colourful market characters. Let our final glimpse of him be as he stands chatting with the traders as they dismantle their stalls on a fine summer's evening, not so very long ago.

Notes

1 Thomas Simmons senior was baptized 1 December 1814 at Little Clacton. Sarah Moor was born 2 September 1818 at Boxted, and baptized there 11 October. They married 7 May 1844 at Little Clacton Parish Church, and both signed with a cross.

2 Harold Smith, in his introduction to *A History of the Parish of Havering-atte-Bower*, states the name 'Havering' probably derives from the Saxon 'Haveringas' meaning the descendants and followers of the chieftain 'Haver' and subsequently came to mean the place in which they settled. The word 'Bower', Smith suggests, referred originally to the Queen's bed-chamber at the manor of Havering, and was subsequently used as a name for the house itself and later for the village surrounding it.

3 Charles Hussey's article 'All Human Life was There', from *Romford Market 1247–1997, a Romford Recorder Souvenir* (1997, p. 5).

4 The poem is printed in full in *Romford Miscellany 2*, compiled by I G Sparkes (1970).

5 From the pamphlet *The Congregational Church Romford 1662–1962*: 'Although the 1877 building had been insured for only £2,000, appeals for help to other churches brought in the necessary money not only for a new church but also for a lecture hall and other rooms' (p. 23). The lecture hall was named the Carlisle Institute in memory of the Reverend Samuel Hanna Carlisle, a notable previous Congregational minister in Romford.

6 An advertisement for the job of manager of the sewage farm in *The Times* on 6 March 1885 states that the post came with 'a first-rate residence on the farm with four cottages, cowhouse and other suitable buildings, and large garden'.

7 The River Rom changes its name to the Beam as it passes southwards through Hornchurch down to the Thames. It formed the western boundary of the Liberty of Havering, and now divides the London Boroughs of Havering and Barking & Dagenham.

8 Peritonitis, an inflammation of the peritoneum (the tissue lining the wall of the abdomen and covering the abdominal organs) was invariably fatal at that time. Bullet wounds to the abdomen are difficult to treat even today. In order for a patient to survive, the torn intestines must be thoroughly repaired and antibiotics administered. The patient is fed intravenously and usually also requires a blood transfusion.

9 Background information on the Fenian campaign can be found at www.met.police.uk/history/fenians.htm

10 The inquest jury were listed in the *Essex Weekly News* as John Guyatt, John Loder, Peter Reynolds, J Spencer jun, A Davey, Wm Slipper, Fordham Scruby, Joseph Lake, James Patching, G B Gilbey, John T Pink, W Wallis, and George S Fletcher.

11 Colin Smith's pamphlet *The Story of Romford Common* (1978) states that 'On old maps of the 18th century the area marked for the gallows was somewhere off the Colchester Road near Straight Road. Many an incident of Highway Robbery is recorded in the local registers. Gentlemen of the road were hanged and left in view as a warning to others.'

12 William Philip Allen, Michael O'Brien and Michael Larkin were hanged on 23 November 1867 at New Bailey Prison, Manchester. See Jack Doughty, *The Manchester Outrage* (Jade Publishing, 2003).

13 In May 1856 the trial of Dr William Palmer, accused of murder by poisoning, was removed from Staffordshire, where the crime had been committed, to the Central Criminal Court. Palmer's counsel had successfully argued that the local prejudice against the accused in his home county meant that a fair trial was impossible. A special Act of Parliament (commonly known as Palmer's Act) was required for this unprecedented move.

14 First recorded in 1188, Newgate was rebuilt several times during its long history, the last being in 1783 following its near-destruction by the Gordon rioters. The Central Criminal Court, opened in 1907, and still known as the Old Bailey, now stands on the site.

15 Henry Kemp Avory was the eldest son of Henry Avory, who had been Clerk of the Arraigns at the Central Criminal Court from 1860 until his death in 1881. Coincidentally it was to be Mr Avory's younger brother Horace Edmund who, as Mr Justice Avory, would pass sentence of death upon the murderers of PC George Gutteridge, shot in 1927 on a quiet road a few miles north of Romford.

16 The members of the jury were: John Carpenter, Edward James Fyfield, Charles Spiegelhalter, George Richard Bull, George Hall, Edward Dickens, James Butler, Henry William Budd, William Saunders, Charles Wright, John Seaborne and James Browne.

17 An accused person was eventually allowed to give evidence in their own defence by the Criminal Evidence Act of 1898. Interestingly, Sir Henry Bodkin Poland was instrumental in bringing about this change.

18 The Nichol was a relatively small area enclosed by Old Nichol Street, Mount Street, Virginia Row and Boundary Street, lying just east of Shoreditch High Street. The Reverend Arthur Osborne Jay, who worked there during the 1880s, stated that its population of some 8,000 had a death rate four times greater than the rest of London. The Nichol was eventually razed to the ground to be replaced by the Boundary Estate, officially opened by the Prince of Wales in 1900. Its history has been documented recently by Sarah Wise in *The Blackest Streets: The Life and Death of a Victorian Slum* (2008).

19 Information from a lecture given in February 1977 by Sir John Burgess (grandson of John Burgess) to the local history society at Tullie House in Carlisle.

20 A letter was sent to a local newspaper in 1957 by a man in South Africa who stated that as a young child he had seen 'Mr Summers' jump from the train. A copy of the letter was donated by Sir John Burgess to the Jackson Library collection, Carlisle Library.

Sources and Further Reading

Primary Sources

Essex Record Office, Chelmsford

We made extensive use of the Essex Constabulary staffing records (J/P 2). The Merit Star file is at J/P 2/7. We also drew upon the Liberty of Havering Quarter Sessions documents (Q/HF and Q/HM). The request by Simmons for repairs to the Court House chimney and drains can be found at Q/HF 394. His letter suggesting the removal of the Police Office is at Q/HM 3.

The National Archives, Kew

We consulted prison registers for Pentonville (PCOM 2/73–80); Newgate (PCOM 2/214–21) and Parkhurst (PCOM 2/59). The Pentonville prisoner photograph albums are at PCOM 2/98–104.

We viewed male convict licences and (where available) their indexes within PCOM 6, and criminal registers within HO 27. Material on the case against Adams and Dredge was, unfortunately, scanty, as police reports and witness depositions do not seem to have survived. The charge is at CRIM 6/16 and the calendar of prisoners at CRIM 9/31. The depositions in the case against Rudge, Martin and Baker can be found at ASSI 52/7.

Newspapers and periodicals

We have chiefly used reports from: the *Essex Times, Essex Chronicle, Illustrated Police News, Essex Weekly News, Romford Times, The Times, Carlisle Journal* and *Carlisle Patriot*. Other newspapers and journals consulted are mentioned in the text and notes.

Family history sources

We made extensive use of birth, marriage and death certificates, parish registers and census returns.

Online sources

www.oldbaileyonline.org – Proceedings of the Old Bailey 1674–1913.
http://archive.timesonline.co.uk – The Times Online Archive 1785–1985.
www.oxforddnb.com – Dictionary of National Biography.
www.british-history.ac.uk/source.aspx?pubid=277 –Victoria County History of the County of Essex, vol. 7, ed. W R Powell (1978).
www.essex.police.uk/memorial/images/roll_sim.jpg – The Essex Police Memorial Trust Book of Remembrance, page on Thomas Simmons.

Secondary Sources

Cobb, Belton, *Murdered on Duty: A Chronicle of the Killing of Policemen* (1961). The first modern account of the Simmons case, but not a reliable one.
Frost, Ken, 'The Inspector Simmons Murder, 1885', *Romford Record*, 18 (1986), 5–8.
Scollan, Maureen, 'An Inspector Dies', *The Essex Police Magazine* (1977). A revised version of this groundbreaking essay can be viewed online at: www.essex.police.uk/ memorial/roll_sim.htm
Tait, Lynn, *The Boobing Bobby* is to be found as a cutting in the file on Sergeant Chase in Essex Police Museum in Chelmsford (no publication details supplied).

The following essays are from the highly recommended Essex Police Museum History Notebooks series, and are all available online:
www.essex.police.uk/offbeat/o_mu_51.php – Fred Feather, 'The Cumbrian Link'.
www.essex.police.uk/offbeat/o_mu_29.php – Fred Feather, 'The Amateur Hangman'.
www.essex.police.uk/offbeat/o_mu_17.php – Martyn Lockwood, 'The Rise and Fall of Alfred John Marden'.

Further Reading

Ballard, E G: *Our Old Romford and District* (1981)

Burgoyne, Joan: *Weeley and Weeley Heath: A Pictorial History* (1999)

Evans, Brian: *Bygone Romford* (1988)

Evans, Brian: *Romford Heritage* (2002)

Evans, Brian: *Romford: A History* (2006)

Gray, Adrian: *Crime and Criminals in Victorian Essex* (1988)

Herber, Mark: *Criminal London* (2002)

Roberts, Sally: *Romford in the Nineteenth Century* (1969)

Scollan, Maureen: *Sworn to Serve: Police in Essex* (1993)

Tabrum, Burnett: *A Short History of the Essex Constabulary* (1911)

Terry, George: *Memories of Old Romford* (1880)

Torry, J G: *Chelmsford Prison* (1980)

Woodgate, John: *The Essex Police* (1985)

Index